C000066343

January–Apri

Day by Day
with
God

Rooting women's lives in the Bible

The Bible Reading Fellowship
Christina Press
Abingdon/Tunbridge Wells

The Bible Reading Fellowship
15 The Chambers, Vineyard
Abingdon OX14 3FE
brf.org.uk

The Bible Reading Fellowship (BRF) is a Registered Charity (233280)

ISBN 978 0 85746 766 9

Distributed in Australia by:
MediaCom Education Inc, PO Box 610, Unley, SA 5061
Tel: 1 800 811 311 | admin@mediacom.org.au

Distributed in New Zealand by:
Scripture Union Wholesale, PO Box 760, Wellington
Tel: 04 385 0421 | suwholesale@clear.net.nz

Acknowledgements
Scripture quotations taken from The Holy Bible, New International Version (Anglicised edition) copyright © 1979, 1984, 2011 by Biblica. Used by permission of Hodder & Stoughton Publishers, a Hachette UK company. All rights reserved. 'NIV' is a registered trademark of Biblica. UK trademark number 1448790. • Scripture taken from the Holy Bible, New International Reader's Version®. Copyright © 1996, 1998 Biblica. All rights reserved throughout the world. Used by permission of Biblica. • Scripture quotations from The New Revised Standard Version of the Bible, Anglicised edition, copyright © 1989, 1995 by the Division of Christian Education of the National Council of the Churches of Christ in the United States of America. Used by permission. All rights reserved. • Scripture quotations taken from the Holy Bible, English Standard Version, published by HarperCollins Publishers, © 2001 Crossway Bibles, a division of Good News Publishers. Used by permission. All rights reserved. • Scripture quotations taken from the Holy Bible, New Living Translation, copyright © 1996, 2004, 2007, 2013. Used by permission of Tyndale House Publishers, Inc., Carol Stream, Illinois 60188. All rights reserved. • Scripture taken from the New Century Version®. Copyright © 2005 by Thomas Nelson. Used by permission. All rights reserved. • Extracts from the Authorised Version of the Bible (The King James Bible), the rights in which are vested in the Crown, are reproduced by permission of the Crown's Patentee, Cambridge University Press.

Every effort has been made to trace and contact copyright owners for material used in this resource. We apologise for any inadvertent omissions or errors, and would ask those concerned to contact us so that full acknowledgement can be made in the future.

A catalogue record for this book is available from the British Library

Printed by Gutenberg Press, Tarxien, Malta

Day by Day with God

Edited by **Ali Herbert** and **Jill Rattle**   January–April 2019

Writers in this issue

Rosemary Green has four adult offspring and 14 grandchildren. She and her husband live in Abingdon, where she is mainly involved in ministry among older people in her local church. Her book on prayer ministry, *God's Catalyst*, is published by the Christina Press. *In Touch with God* was written with her husband, Michael.

Helen Williams has worked in music, education, management consultancy and administration. She currently finds herself working mostly alongside her husband, an Anglican bishop, in some fabulously diverse contexts, while continuing to work as an accompanist.

Rachel Turner is the Parenting for Faith Pioneer at BRF. Over the past 15 years, she has worked across a variety of denominations as a children's, youth and family life pastor. She is the author of five books. See **parentingforfaith.org**.

Ann Warren began her career in the BBC as a producer and scriptwriter, subsequently training as a pastoral counsellor and life coach. She was a regular Christian Viewpoint speaker and has written a number of books including her personal story of healing in *No Place to Belong*.

Tania Vaughan is a ministerial student at Bristol Baptist College. She is passionate about teaching God's word and helping women deepen their relationship with God. She has written a number of online devotional studies and is the author of *Let's Talk About Sex and Relationships*, a study for single Christian women.

Victoria Byrne is a pastor for seniors at her Twickenham church and loves encouraging others. She is currently co-writing a book of Indian recipes and life stories.

Chine McDonald is Head of Christian Influence and Engagement at World Vision UK, and a trustee of the Sophia Network, Church and Media Network, Greenbelt and Christians Against Poverty. She is a regular contributor to the BBC's *Thought for the Day*, *Daily Service*, *Pause for Thought* and *Prayer for the Day*.

Amy Boucher Pye is a writer and speaker who runs the *Woman Alive* book club. She's the author of the award-winning *Finding Myself in Britain* (Authentic, 2015) and *The Living Cross* (BRF, 2016). Find her at **amyboucherpye.com**.

Sandra Wheatley had a distinguished career in nursing, served as a missionary and was in full-time ministry before MS brought an enforced change and the emergence of a more contemplative life, called to prayer and intercession. She lives in north-east England.

Sheila Jacobs is a writer, editor and award-winning author of eleven novels, including *Watchers* (2003/2009). She has also written nonfiction. Her latest book is *To Live Again* (DLT, 2017). She lives in north Essex, attends an Elim church where she is currently serving as a deacon, and is also a day chaplain at a retreat centre.

Jill Rattle and Ali Herbert write...

Happy New Year and welcome to the first issue of *Day by Day with God* 2019! Whatever your experience of last year, with all its challenges and joys, the beginning of a new year is always a good time to stop and take stock personally, practically and spiritually, seeing where God has been at work in our lives and how he might be longing to transform us in these coming months.

In this issue, you will travel with us from winter to spring, which in itself is a picture of the transforming work of our wonderful God who draws us from death towards life in all its fullness. At the opening of the year, Rosemary Green reminds us of all the ways God is 'God of the new', inviting us to recommit ourselves to the walk of faith at the very start of the year – and to continue to refresh that commitment as we journey onwards. In the closing notes, we will enter in once again to the miraculous Easter story and the days following, as Sheila Jacobs explores the newness of resurrection life. Let's be expectant that we will all experience the renewal God has to offer.

We are thrilled to introduce Rachel Turner as one of our new writers. Rachel has worked as a family and children's pastor for many years, helping parents engage their children in a life of faith. She will be taking a lively look at the book of Numbers, catching a glimpse of God's heart and particularly looking at the challenges of how we might flourish in a season of dryness.

In the process of moving house last year, one of Jill's small worries was finding enough space on the road for the large removal lorry to park – in the heart of a busy city, parking spaces come at a premium! Making space for anything in our busy lives is often difficult, and making space for God is something many of us struggle with. And yet, nothing in our lives is more important than making space for him. We believe God is pleased that you have made the decision to create space 'day by day' to encounter him, to find him in his word, to hear what he wants to say to you. As 2019 begins, remember that because you are seeking him, you will definitely find him. That is his promise.

New!

Rosemary Green writes:

We are at the beginning of 2019 (where did last year go?). And to think that when I was a child I wondered whether I would even reach the Millennium! I wonder if you make a New Year's resolution – does that phrase have an inbuilt expectation of failure? We might ask instead, what is our fresh commitment to Christ for this year? Not what I think I should be doing; but what does the Lord want of me this year? It is worth writing that down: look at it at the beginning of each month; see how we are measuring up, and renew that commitment regularly. Our son does an annual spiritual stocktaking: he uses his birthday each year to reflect on the past year – its joys and sorrows, its challenges, on accomplishments and failures. We might do a similar thing at the start of each month.

We start this year in our readings thinking of some of the new aspects of our life in Christ. I hope we will be excited as we are reminded of what the Lord has done for us, how he has changed our lives. We begin with a reality that is older than anything in the world – God's love. Psalm 136 reminds us in every verse that 'his love endures forever'. In the words of John Keble's hymn, 'new every morning is the love, our waking and uprising prove.' We can thank God daily for his love.

If we have been Christians for many years, it can be easy to start taking for granted the truths we have known and experienced. I hope that as we look at the 'new' things that God does for us, that staleness will be replaced by freshness. Ask the Lord to blow with the bellows of his Spirit on to the embers of our faith. Pray each day for expectancy, that we will finish our devotional time knowing that we have been renewed in our love for Jesus, in our vigour, in the way we are going to live for him each day. And look for fresh excitement with our wonderful God, and ever-deepening love for him.

New every morning

Because of the Lord's great love we are not consumed, for his compassions never fail. They are new every morning; great is your faithfulness. I say to myself, 'The Lord is my portion; therefore I will wait for him.' (NIV)

By the end of a summer's day, a sandy beach is in a mess: sandcastles, footprints of dogs and their owners, discarded debris... all there, and more. But overnight, the tide comes in, the sand is flattened, the rubbish and seaweed left at high-tide mark or washed away altogether. The beach starts a new day.

I see here a picture of God's utter faithfulness and love. His compassions *never* fail. They are new *every* morning. Jeremiah, the author of Lamentations, is sure of this, despite the affliction and bitterness he refers to in verse 19. The awfulness of his apparently hopeless situation is spelled out in a graphic description of his plight in verses 1–18. It is against that backdrop that he chooses to stop wallowing in his misery. He turns away from saying, 'My splendour is gone and all that I had hoped from the Lord' (v. 18); instead, he concentrates on God's love: 'This I call to mind and therefore I have hope' (v. 21). It is similar in many of the psalms, where we see a clear, decisive choice to turn from misery and depression to focus on God and his faithfulness. Psalm 69 is one of my favourites, because of the powerful way the Lord used it to pick me up. Verses 1–12 are full of despair; verse 13 has the turning point, 'But I pray to you, Lord.'

So what do you expect of 2019? As far as you can tell, is your life likely to remain stable? Or do you face some big changes of job, location, family events of births, marriages, deaths, children leaving home? And what about the unexpected? Are you excited or fearful (or a mixture of both)? Whatever 2019 brings, we can be sure of God's faithfulness and love, 365 days, as sure as the tide.

Give thanks for each new day in the words of John Keble's hymn. 'New mercies, each returning day... New dangers past, new sins forgiven, new thoughts of God, new hopes of heaven.'

ROSEMARY GREEN

A new heart

'I will give you a new heart and put a new spirit in you; I will remove from you your heart of stone and give you a heart of flesh. And I will put my Spirit in you and move you to follow my decrees.' (NIV)

I used to think of these verses just as a promise to individuals, but I was wrong; that is the danger of taking Bible verses out of context. God is speaking to the Israelite nation, a people in exile. Their conquest by the Babylonians and their deportation was an act of human aggression. But it was also God's judgement on their corruption. Look, for example, at the behaviour of king, priests and people in 2 Chronicles 36:11–4, and Jeremiah's comment: 'It was because of the Lord's anger that all this happened to Jerusalem and Judah, and in the end he thrust them from his presence' (Jeremiah 52:3).

We tend to go soft nowadays on God's holy judgement. But recognising that aspect of his character leads to a fuller appreciation of his love, his mercy and his forgiveness. Some half-century after the judgement of exile, Ezekiel writes of God's promise to do a new thing in his people, to give them a new heart and a new spirit, leading to new attitudes and new obedience.

As I look round at our own nation, I see how far and how fast we are moving from our Christian heritage. God is largely ignored, even if people believe in his existence, and some of our laws are no longer founded on the principles of the ten commandments. Will you join me in committing to pray for God to do a new thing in our nation, to give us a new heart and a new spirit?

But of course a nation is made up of individuals. If a nation is going to change, individual stony hearts that disregard God need his heart surgery. He wants each person to receive the new heart of love and compassion that he offers, and to embrace his Spirit, so that we want, and are able, to obey him.

Thank you, Lord, for the new heart you have given me. Please help me to pray with concern, insight and compassion for a nation in deep need.

ROSEMARY GREEN

A new birth

Jesus answered, 'Very truly I tell you, no one can enter the kingdom of God unless they are born of water and the Spirit. Flesh gives birth to flesh, but the Spirit gives birth to spirit. You should not be surprised at my saying, "You must be born again."' (NIV)

Nicodemus was intrigued by Jesus. A leading Pharisee, an aristocratic member of the Sanhedrin, he dared not lose face by being seen talking with Jesus, so he crept in under cover of darkness. He had seen enough of Jesus to affirm that here was someone special from God. He was already puzzled. He was even more puzzled when Jesus began to speak of a second birth. Nicodemus didn't need to turn over a new leaf; he needed to get a new life. 'Flesh gives birth to flesh' (v. 6): human birth happens when the sperm enters the egg and fertilises it. For the new spirit birth, the Holy Spirit enters our inner being to fertilise it for this second birth, just as we were reading yesterday of God's promise through Ezekiel of a new heart and a new spirit.

I grew up in a traditional Anglican home, with somewhat erratic churchgoing. I never doubted as a historical fact Jesus' virgin birth, his miracles, death, resurrection and ascension. But it was all 2,000 years ago and made little impact on my life. A sermon on Zacchaeus was a revelation. First, I saw that I was not a cut above everyone else ('Zacchaeus – Rosemary – come down'), and that brought me to see how much I needed the forgiveness Jesus bought for me on the cross. Second, I understood that his resurrection meant he was alive to be my friend. And, like Zacchaeus, I needed to invite Jesus' Spirit into my life. Initially, that seemed too simple a step, but as soon as I did – wow! Life changed! I didn't understand this new birth, but I knew it was true. I had a new perspective on life, wanting to read the Bible, to pray, to learn from other Christians. It was a new birth indeed. What about yours?

Do you want your friends and relations to know this new life? Ask God to show you a few individuals to concentrate on in regular, expectant, patient prayer for their new birth.

ROSEMARY GREEN

A new relationship

'The days are coming,' declares the Lord, 'when I will make a new covenant with the people of Israel… No longer will they teach their neighbour, or say to one another, "Know the Lord," because they will all know me, from the least of them to the greatest.' (NIV)

A new heart, a new birth and now a new covenant and a new relationship. However long we have been Christians, I hope we never lose the wonder at the infinite, holy God's rescue plan for us puny, sinful mortals.

Jeremiah was writing 600 years before Jesus came, but God's 'new' plan to restore humankind's broken relationship with himself had been set far back in eternity. 'They will all know me, from the least of them to the greatest' (v. 34). This privilege of knowing him was not to be confined to the priests, to the rich or aristocratic, to the educated, nor even to the people of Israel. 'They will all know me.' That is the privilege that you and I have under the new covenant.

How is this new relationship possible? The last verse of today's reading gives us the answer: God's forgiveness dissolves the barrier that human sin puts between ourselves and a holy God, whose 'eyes are too pure to look on evil' and who 'cannot tolerate wrongdoing' (Habakkuk 1:13).

I love the way our hands can demonstrate the way Jesus took on himself the world's wrongdoing. Place a weight on one hand, then hold both hands towards the light. One hand represents Jesus; nothing separates him from God's light. The other hand with a heavy weight represents me. Now transfer the weight to the 'Jesus hand'. Isaiah said, 'The Lord has laid on him the iniquity of us all' (Isaiah 53:6). I am free to know God; I am freely forgiven because Jesus takes all our sin on himself on the cross. Momentarily, his relationship with God is broken ('My God, why have you forsaken me?') so that ours with God is restored.

Thank you, Father, that you are a holy, forgiving God, and for the immense privilege of knowing you.

ROSEMARY GREEN

A new hunger

Like newborn babies, you should long for the pure milk of God's word. It will help you grow up as believers. You can do this now that you have tasted how good the Lord is. (NIRV)

I'm staying in a home where there are three-week-old puppies. There is much squealing and squawking as they clamour for food – first for their mother's milk, then later for the more solid food. Those puppies can teach us, in their eagerness for food which satisfies their hunger and helps them to grow. In my early years as a Christian, I was eager to learn. I took any opportunities I could to be nourished by fellowship, by Bible reading (alone and in participatory study groups), by prayer, by Christian service (sometimes tactless, in my youthful enthusiasm to tell others the good news). In later years, I regret to say, middle-aged complacency has lost some of that early zeal (unlike the puppies' mother, as eager for food as she ever was). But I know that there is no substitute for regular, expectant Bible reading for spiritual nourishment.

Alongside a healthy diet, we must make sure we are not eating the junk food of gossip and resentment. 'Rid yourselves of all malice and all deceit, hypocrisy, envy and slander' (v. 1, NIV): those are all poison. 'Rid yourselves' – that speaks of determined action. Thoughts, attitudes, words: all may need a spring cleaning, so that love, truth and sincerity prevail. Those qualities will be nurtured as we discard the poison, as we 'pray in' scripture and let the Holy Spirit make changes in us.

One more thought: if you are in the privileged position of caring for another newborn believer, think of a baby who moves slowly from milk, to puree, to more solid food. I am so grateful for the older Christian who helped me into church and a small group, answered my many questions, showed me how to read the Bible and to pray, and ensured that I was clear about basics of belief and behaviour. Can you do this for someone you know?

Jesus said, 'My food… is to do the will of him who sent me and to finish his work' (John 4:34, NIV). Ponder this thought of being nourished by whole-hearted obedience to God.

ROSEMARY GREEN

A new power

We were therefore buried with him through baptism into death in order that, just as Christ was raised from the dead through the glory of the Father, we too may live a new life. (NIV)

Paul is excited! He longs for his readers to grasp the confidence and joy they – and we – can have with our new life in Christ. In previous chapters, he has argued painstakingly that our right standing with God does not depend on an impossible 100% obedience to the old law, but on his mercy and grace which we grasp through our faith in Christ. This is not to be an excuse for 'more sin, so more grace'. Rather, it is an incentive to enter fully into the fruit of Jesus' death and resurrection. He is saying, 'Come on, people; put the past behind; live your new life to the full in the power of the resurrection.'

Years ago, I visited the Anglican cathedral in Colombo, Sri Lanka. I was very struck by the large baptistry immediately inside the main door. Down several steps into the water, up steps the other side. I saw a powerful symbol of the meaning of baptism – die to sin, rise to life in Christ.

Do you notice the repeated themes in these verses? Verses 4–6, 8 and 11 all speak of our being united with Christ in his death. I find 'our old self was crucified with him' the most powerful phrase. Paul emphasises the link between Jesus' death and resurrection, which we find in verses 4–5 and 8–9. Paul is very intentional here: he speaks directly to me, as I struggle with an addiction to a computer card game. 'Count yourselves dead to sin but alive to God in Christ Jesus' (v. 11). 'Rosemary, Christ died so you can be free from that addiction, no longer a slave to it.' Our faith is a practical one; historical events 2,000 years ago can be worked out in our lives today.

Your battles will be different from mine. But together we can pray Paul's prayer in Ephesians 1:18–21, that we know for ourselves the 'incomparably great power' that raised Jesus from the dead.

ROSEMARY GREEN

A new lifestyle

Do not lie to one another, seeing that you have stripped off the old self with its practices and have clothed yourselves with the new self, which is being renewed in knowledge according to the image of its creator. (NRSV)

'Take off, put on.' I like the image of a shabby old coat being discarded in favour of a brand-new jacket. Of course, Paul is talking about something more fundamental than an outer garment. It is our inner selves that are being changed, 'the new self'. But we have a part to play in this transformation. As Paul says in Philippians 2:12–13: 'Work out your own salvation… for it is God who is at work in you.' We must cooperate with him, so that the evidence of inner change is seen in our behaviour and attitude.

'Put to death.' That's a strong command. I think of the TV advert about the weeds, mocking the discouraged owner – who then sprays them with his powerful weedkiller, so they shrivel overnight. Sadly, the weeds of sin don't disappear as quickly the advert portrays (though I heard a testimony recently of a young woman whose bad language and swearing stopped as soon as she became a Christian). Our thought lives, sex lives, anger and dishonesty are among the weeds which must be killed. Big sins, small sins; they all matter. In their place, the flowers of compassion, kindness, humility, gentleness and patience will be able to flourish.

Key to this is our willingness to forgive whatever grievance we may have against another person, however badly they have wronged us. Resentments are like cancer: without treatment, they are fatal. We may not feel like forgiving or letting go; we may not want to. But if we want to please Jesus, we follow both his example of forgiveness on the cross and his teaching. Remember the parable of the unforgiving servant in Matthew 18:21–35? Verses 34–35 show the anger of the master who threw his servant into prison, illustrating the judgement of the Father on those who will not forgive.

'Love covers a multitude of sins' (1 Peter 4:8). His love blots out my hidden and visible sins.

ROSEMARY GREEN

A new song

I waited patiently for the Lord; he turned to me and heard my cry. He lifted me out of the slimy pit, out of the mud and mire; he set my feet on a rock and gave me a firm place to stand. He put a new song in my mouth. (NIV)

When did you last feel you were in an insecure place? David's description of a slimy pit, of mud and mire, is graphic. We sense a slippery foothold, we're unable to move forward safely.

What a contrast with the solidity of a rock on which to stand! I picture Jesus' strong hand reaching down to grasp, firmly but gently, the slipping person and lift them on to the rock. Pause, and imagine yourself sliding around, calling out for help. Then 'feel' a strong hand picking you up, placing you securely on a firm, flat rock. A relieved sigh of thanks is followed by jubilant praise, with a song and a testimony that leads others to trust God as well.

Before you read any further, stop to think what you would include in your own song of thanks and praise... Now we turn back to the psalm to see what David includes. First, he trusts a reliable God, not any man who, in pride, trusts in his own abilities. Nor does he trust any false god. That leads me to ask myself if the Lord is first in my life at all times. Then he thinks of the multitude of good things God has done for him (v. 5). I remember Jeremiah 29:11: 'I know the plans I have for you,' says the Lord, 'plans to prosper you and not to harm you, plans to give you a hope and a future.' Thank you, Lord.

Verses 6–8 remind us that the Lord is more interested in our loving obedience than in outward forms of observance. The opened (or 'pierced') ears refer to the slave who loves the family he serves and chooses to remain a slave for life. Finally (verses 9–10), we are not to be secret believers but to speak unashamedly of God's love, truth and salvation.

Psalms 96 and 98 both start 'Sing to the Lord a new song.' Join in one of these exuberant psalms by reading it slowly, aloud if possible, pausing to savour each verse.

ROSEMARY GREEN

A new commandment

'A new command I give you: love one another. As I have loved you, so you must love one another. By this everyone will know that you are my disciples, if you love one another.' (NIV)

Love one another. Three simple words – but a key to life, a key to experiencing God, a key to portraying Jesus to the world.

'As I have loved you.' That is the standard he set for us. 'Greater love has no one than this: to lay down one's life for one's friends' (John 15:13). That is how much Jesus loves us. Even though we cannot match his sacrificial love, other people can be attracted by the warmth and love of our fellowship.

I grew up not knowing much about the real quality of love. Then, when I had been a Christian for 25 years, I realised how little I knew about loving other people. I read Paul's chapter on love in 1 Corinthians 13, and prayed through gritted teeth, 'Lord, please give me that love.' One hand was open, the other clenched tight: 'If I had that love, I would have to give more to other people and receive from them', and I wasn't ready for that. I was stuck in that half-and-half place for a year; then, with a husband in hospital in South Africa with meningitis and me in England, I had to let down my barriers of independence and allow other people to love me in very practical ways. As I received God's love through them, it was planted in me. It took root, and loving other people became a joy, not a chore.

At the end of today's reading, we read Peter's impulsive promise to follow Jesus anywhere. 'You mean well,' says Jesus, 'but in the next few hours, you will deny knowing me' – Peter's failure of love. We followers of Jesus often fail to love; Jesus never does.

Ponder John's words: 'Dear children, let us not love with words or speech but with actions and in truth' (1 John 3:18). Lord, may I listen, and act.

ROSEMARY GREEN

A new covenant

He has made us competent as ministers of a new covenant – not of the letter but of the Spirit; for the letter kills, but the Spirit gives life. (NIV)

An exciting new day has dawned – new covenant, new promises, new relationship, new assurance of forgiveness. The new covenant, promised through Jeremiah (31:31–34) about 600BC, arrived with Jesus. On the last night of his life, he presided at the Passover meal with his disciples: 'After the supper he took the cup, saying, "This cup is the new covenant in my blood, which is poured out for you"' (Luke 22:20). The old covenant was a covenant of law and obedience, based on, 'If you will, then I will…' The old covenant was a necessary stepping stone to understanding God and his ways, and humankind's relationship with him. It educated, but it could not redeem.

The new covenant brings freedom and assurance; it is a covenant of forgiveness, and of obedience born of love, not of duty. As Jesus said, 'If you love me, keep my commands' (John 14:15). Through the new covenant, the Holy Spirit is released in our lives – that Spirit who enables us to win the inner tug-of-war between the downward pull of our old sinful nature and the new desire to please Jesus wholeheartedly. 'We all, who with unveiled faces contemplate the Lord's glory, are being transformed into his image with ever-increasing glory, which comes from the Lord, who is the Spirit' (v. 18). That's pretty exciting!

In the early days of charismatic renewal in the 1960s, my own spiritual life was very shrivelled; I was suspicious of what seemed to be the over-the-top Christians, and scared of their X-ray eyes that I felt pierced through to my emptiness. But God used that time of Michael's meningitis to fill me with his Spirit in a way I had never known. The change I experienced was as transforming as the day of my new birth, 25 years earlier.

Lord, thank you so much for the power of the life-giving Spirit through the new covenant. And thank you for your faithfulness, even when it seems a long time between promise and fulfilment.

ROSEMARY GREEN

A new heaven and a new earth

Then I saw 'a new heaven and a new earth,' for the first heaven and the first earth had passed away, and there was no longer any sea… And I heard a loud voice from the throne saying, 'Look! God's dwelling-place is now among the people, and he will dwell with them.' (NIV)

So far, we have thought of the many new blessings in our life with Christ as we know it now. But what will it be like in eternity? Well, I haven't been there, so I don't really know! But I notice some of the phrases that John uses, and try to get a glimpse of something that is far, far outside my experience of life here on earth, more wonderful than I can ever imagine.

John paints a picture of unimaginable beauty, radiance and perfection. Earlier in Revelation he wrote of the worship in heaven, with the throne of God, with One sitting on it, with the Lamb of God in the centre. The church, the 'bride of Christ', shines with the glory of God. Paul wrote of the completeness that will come. 'Now I know in part; then I shall know fully, even as I am fully known' (1 Corinthians 13:12). We have thought of the privilege we have of knowing God, here and now. But that relationship is a pale imitation of the 'knowing' we will have in eternity.

A new heaven, and a new earth – the earth as it was meant to be before the fall, a world that is unspoilt. Paul wrote of the 'hope that the creation itself will be liberated from its bondage to decay and brought into the freedom and glory of the children of God' (Romans 8:20–21). It will be a world without sin and without pain. There will be nothing to spoil it. Satan is gone for ever, 'thrown into a lake of burning sulphur' (Revelation 20:10). Just what it will be like, I don't pretend to know. But I am sure that God and his people will be in an eternal relationship of pure love.

Father, I'm finite and out of my depth. But I am privileged to know you, even dimly, now; and I look forward to this unknown, marvellous future.

ROSEMARY GREEN

A new creation

Therefore, if anyone is in Christ, the new creation has come: the old has gone, the new is here! All this is from God, who reconciled us to himself through Christ and gave us the ministry of reconciliation: that God was reconciling the world to himself in Christ. (NIV)

'The new creation has come.' We are not yet at that final point in history of the new heavens and new earth we were thinking about yesterday; but we have seen since 1 January some of the treasures and privileges of the new life in Christ.

We are meant to enjoy this new life. But we are not meant to be selfish by keeping it to ourselves. As Paul says here, we are ambassadors for God. We are his representatives in a foreign country. And we have extraordinarily good news to share: the news of God's unfailing love and of the new things he does in us. If I say that we have a duty to tell others, it sounds dull and heavy. But if I am excited about Jesus, I will not want to keep it to myself; I will want to bubble over with the good news. Our daughter-in-law recently heard she is to be a grandmother. She found it very hard to keep quiet about it for three weeks!

In a totally different situation, I have a friend in an eastern European country who, with three others, is accused of breaking the law by their public witness for Jesus; they long for other people to hear about him in their very secular country. (I am praying that this alarming situation will actually give them fresh opportunities for witness.)

We can find plenty of excuses to keep quiet about our faith – ignorance, 'not the right time', fear of rejection and many others. I am not a 'natural' evangelist (in comparison to my husband, who is), but I am aware that I may be the only Christian known to some of my friends and acquaintances. How can I best show them that Jesus is good news for them?

Lord, thank you for the good news of new life with you. Please remind me to start each day with a prayer that I will have the chance to put in a word for you.

ROSEMARY GREEN

A woodland walk

Helen Williams writes:

I have just been for my first walk in six weeks! As I write, it's a chill November afternoon but I was overjoyed to be out after being cooped up 'resting' following surgery. I didn't manage to get far but I was privileged to see burnt-orange sycamores and velvet green yews in the churchyard; willows either side of a bubbling stream; an egret taking flight from one of them and flapping elegantly to land on the adjacent watercress beds. I saw beech trees whose leaves had turned every shade of red, orange, yellow, gold and brown next to the bare branches of horse chestnut and ash. I saw scarlet-berried holly trees and the silhouettes of pine trees against the sunset sky and, on my return to the garden, one or two of my young apple trees were still proffering fruit.

What an extraordinary world God has made – such variety and colour and texture!

You will be reading this in January when leaf-shedding trees are most likely to be bare, or almost bare. I am, nevertheless, going to invite you to come on a woodland walk with me. It will be a walk through the seasons and sometimes you may need to use your imagination, especially if you live in a place where there are no trees. Along the way, let's see what the Bible says about trees and how Jesus, the carpenter who worked with wood, observed and used them to illustrate his teaching. We will listen in on some encounters in and under trees and, perhaps most import-antly of all, reflect on the overarching story of salvation as seen in the link between the Trees of Life and of the Knowledge of Good and Evil in Eden, the tree on which Jesus died and the Tree of Life (mentioned in both Ezekiel and Revelation with its breathtaking leaves 'for the healing of the nations').

In 1 Kings 4, the multilayered nature of Solomon's wisdom is described. I find it fascinating that one of the facets of his wisdom was that he 'spoke about plant life, from the cedar of Lebanon to the hyssop that grows out of walls'! May God give us too more of his wisdom as we look at the nature of life itself over these next 14 days and, along the way, may we, as one of my favourite poets writes, 'bathe in his fall-gold mercies'.

The proud cedar tree

[The cedar] was majestic in beauty, with its spreading boughs, for its roots went down to abundant waters. The cedars in the garden of God could not rival it, nor could the junipers equal its boughs, nor could the plane trees compare with its branches. (NIV)

Before we visit the garden of Eden, let's look together at this beautiful allegory in Ezekiel. The huge cedar tree represents Assyria, and the inherent warning not to become arrogant or proud is for Pharaoh. A wonderful description of a tree (vv. 2–9) is followed by the story of what may happen when pride takes over and God withdraws his care and protection. This is, of course, an Old Testament warning to a superpower, but there is resonance enough for us.

I used to have a lovely Labrador whom I often walked in our local woods. The first part of the circuit was down a narrow drovers' road with trees grown into an overhead arch. It might sound strange, but I would use this natural tunnel at the start of my walk as my confession time. The walk took me to places of praise, inspiration and intercession too, but it was helpful to start with 'sorry'. It might be good, as we begin this woodland journey, to confess any pride and tendency we have to self-reference, handing to God the people or things we have allowed to take his place. Let's allow him to restore us to the beauty of that nourished, thriving tree.

I also wanted to remind you of Moses' desert encounter with God. I hope you'll forgive me for introducing a burning 'bush' and not a tree. (According to several commentators, it was probably a small acacia tree Moses saw!) Trees play such a significant role in reducing erosion, moderating climate, removing carbon dioxide from the atmosphere and storing large quantities of carbon in their tissues, not to mention all their obvious uses as habitats and for wood and food production. In Exodus 3, though, a tree is something even greater: a place of encounter with God.

As we journey with you, Lord, through the woods and gardens of the Bible, please show us more of yourself. May we see with clarity, hear with understanding and receive with a grateful heart as we encounter you.

HELEN WILLIAMS

Pleasing to the eye and good for food

The Lord God made all kinds of trees grow out of the ground – trees that were pleasing to the eye and good for food. (NIV)

God's creation of trees is such a perfect expression of himself as creator: he creates them both for a function – to bear fruit for food – but also for aesthetic reasons – just for our pleasure. It is maybe no coincidence that the Hebrew word 'eden' means 'delight'. You can imagine the ultimate Artist setting out to design the earth's landscapes – huge oaks, majestic sequoias, graceful willows and delicate Japanese maples, as well as edible fruit-producing palms, apple trees, olive trees and a myriad more. There is extravagance, colour, shape and texture in his design, and you have only to think of trees like the baobab, with its topsy-turvy look, to realise that there is humour at work too.

The psalmist speaks of the creation of trees in Psalm 104, singing of the cedars of Lebanon planted and watered by the Lord, in which the birds of the air make nests, and of the juniper tree, which provides a home for the stork.

In Ezekiel 17:22–24, God speaks of planting a tree from a shoot, tending it and making it grow so tall it will provide shade and also a home for birds. If you have time to look, you will see that these verses remind us that he holds all things in balance and that he has the power to make the lowly lofty and the mighty weak, whether trees or people. He is the creator and sustainer of life.

It may be mid-January, but see if you can find time to get out and look, really look, at a tree. If there are no trees near you or you can't get out, maybe a photograph on the internet or in a book would help. Spend some time just marvelling at the diversity and richness of the trees God has created.

'God writes the gospel not in the Bible alone, but also on trees, and in the flowers and clouds and stars,' wrote Martin Luther. Ask God to speak to you today through his astonishing creation.

HELEN WILLIAMS

Midwinter roots

I pray that you, being rooted and established in love, may have power... to grasp how wide and long and high and deep is the love of Christ, and to know this love that surpasses knowledge – that you may be filled to the measure of all the fullness of God. (NIV)

'Let us learn to appreciate there will be times when the trees will be bare, and look forward to the time when we may pick the fruit,' said Chekhov. It's midwinter but, as we embark upon our woodland walk, it's a day to pause and wonder what's happening to these bare trees underground. If you get the chance to look at a tree today, do. If you're unable to see one but have access to the internet, why not look up David Hockney's picture, *Three Trees near Thixendale* (the winter one)?

Trees 'extend impressively in both directions, up and down, shearing rock and fanning air, doing their real business just out of reach,' writes Annie Dillard. It's in this secret place that so much of the work of growth goes on, large and complex root systems developing, sometimes even during the winter as well. It's a time of 'quiescence' where roots are resting but ready. Thus evergreens, and even many deciduous trees, may expand their root systems in search of water and nutrients before spring buds break.

Paul prays that the Ephesians' roots will be deeply 'established in love' as they contemplate the indescribable nature of God's love for them. We often talk about 'going deeper' with God. What does this really mean? A friend sent me a picture this week of a largely uprooted tree, together with the prayer below. The tree is lying on its side but has many shoots bursting forth from its trunk. Clearly some of its roots stayed rooted, despite whatever trauma it faced, and there is life! Are we so firmly planted, our roots so sunk into Jesus' solidity, absorbing his love, nourished by his teaching, trusting him for every moment of every day – so rooted that nothing can uproot us?

'Lord, storms have stolen the life I had hoped for, so help me to find ways, like this beautiful tree, to thrive despite my brokenness. Help me to grow in ways I never thought possible.'

HELEN WILLIAMS

Myrtle instead of briars

You will go out in joy and be led forth in peace; the mountains and hills will burst into song before you, and all the trees of the field will clap their hands. Instead of the thorn-bush will grow the juniper and instead of briers the myrtle will grow. (NIV)

Continuing our winter journey, there's a tree mentioned in the Bible which is always green and is reported to have such a strong root system it can withstand temperatures of -15°C. In season, it has fragrant flowers and produces berries useful in cooking. Branches of this tree, the myrtle, are used to make the roof of shelters for the Jewish Feast of Tabernacles (Nehemiah 8:14–15) – a time for remembering God's mercy and faithfulness.

The first of Zechariah's eight visions is set in a myrtle grove. For the Jews, myrtle symbolised sweetness, justice, recovery, peace and God's generosity. Zechariah's vision of God, horsemen and angels among the myrtle trees reinforces God's promise that the returned exiles to whom he spoke would be blessed with prosperity.

Here in our passage from Isaiah, the myrtle is also a sign of re-creation and blessing. Isaiah says it will grow where briars used to prevail. It's a wonderful picture of what happens when we leave behind our self-determining ways, turn to God and accept the mercy he simply cannot wait to show (v. 7). It makes little sense to us, but we're reminded that there's no way we are ever really going to understand God's ways or thoughts (vv. 8–9). His love, mercy and promise of forgiveness are to be taken seriously: they lead to joy and peace (v. 12).

Earlier in the Old Testament, in 1 Chronicles 16, Psalms 96 and 148, and in Isaiah 44 too, the trees of the forest are exhorted to 'burst into song' or be 'jubilant' at what God has done. Here, there is a promise that the trees will even 'clap their hands'! I can believe it, having just witnessed the most astonishing sunset – a luminous orange-pink sky, beech trees shimmering in golden light and a vast rainbow arching over them.

Perhaps the myrtle can help us focus on God's promises today: M for Mercy; Y for Yielding (as in crops); R for Re-creation; T for God's Thoughts; L for his Love; and E for the fact that he is Everlasting.

HELEN WILLIAMS

A mustard seed

'The kingdom of heaven is like a mustard seed, which a man took and planted in his field. Though it is the smallest of all seeds, yet when it grows, it is the largest of garden plants and becomes a tree, so that the birds come and perch in its branches.' (NIV)

Although I love gardening, I'm not great at planning ahead. Winter is the time when serious gardeners are, I'm sure, thumbing through seed catalogues and planning what to sow in the spring. Today's reading draws us to the potential of a seed. If you can acquire some mustard seeds to plant and observe as they grow (as some may have done on school blotting paper!), that may be a tangible reminder of this parable's challenge.

The *Brassica Nigra* seed was the smallest seed sown by first-century Palestinian farmers and yet capable of achieving tree status. In the Old Testament, great empires were often depicted as huge trees, with subject nations shown as birds sheltering within their branches (see Ezekiel 31:6). This would have been a powerful illustration of God's kingdom and rule.

Jesus alludes to Isaiah 6, where Isaiah speaks of a significant 'holy seed'. People have waited a long time, but now at last the shoot from this seed is appearing – in the person of Jesus. It's just not what people were expecting, though. There is confusion about Jesus and no comprehension about what God will do through him.

There's a message for us here: are we ready for God to do the unexpected or are we in danger of deciding exactly what God ought to be doing in our lives, our churches and our world, leaving us unable to hear what he's actually saying?

How encouraging that Jesus points to the time when God's rule will be supreme, despite the kingdom's small beginnings. Do you ever wonder how we can make more impact in our world? The Isaiah 6 passage also contains Isaiah's own preparation for ministry where, despite his feelings of total inadequacy, he says to the Lord, 'Here am I. Send me.'

When the fourth-century Antony of Egypt was asked how to please God, he replied: 'Whoever you may be, always have God before your eyes; whatever you do, do it according to the testimony of the Holy Scriptures.'

HELEN WILLIAMS

Recovering greenness

The pastures in the wilderness are becoming green. The trees are bearing their fruit; the fig-tree and the vine yield their riches. Be glad, people of Zion, rejoice in the Lord your God, for he has given you ... spring rains. (NIV)

Our woodland walk brings us today to springtime, which may feel like a long way off. In C.S. Lewis' *The Lion, the Witch and the Wardrobe*, there is a moment when the lion Aslan starts to breathe his life back into Narnia, releasing the ice-bound land from perpetual winter into joyous spring. There is something of that joy here in Joel's prophecy: spring showers, a greening land, fruit and crops in abundance – a proliferation of good things. There is 'abundance', 'riches' and 'plenty' and there are 'wonders'.

First, though, comes God's call to the people of Judah to return to him from their wickedness, in order to escape God's inevitable judgement. He offers them a way out and a chance to really live. Just as the blessings he promises are lavish, so he asks, through Joel, for a genuine, wholehearted 'return' (v. 12), involving a complete change of heart.

There is a poem called 'The Flower' by George Herbert which I have found very helpful over the years. He uses the metaphor of a flower to describe his heart. The poem begins with the flower in springtime: 'Who would have thought my shrivel'd heart could have recover'd greennesse? It was gone quite under ground; as flowers depart to see their mother-root, when they have blown; where they together all the hard weather, dead to the world, keep house unknown.'

Do you ever have that sense of having a shrivelled heart, perhaps not having kept close company with God for some time, or having been through an unusually tough and demanding period? I do. Herbert reminds us that God's springtime is powerful and will lead to the recovery of greenness.

Reading on in Joel 2, God also promises to restore the years devoured by the locust and to pour out his Holy Spirit. What a spring!

(A bare twig with its winter-closed buds may be a useful prompt for prayer today.) Lord, I return to you with all my heart and ask you to breathe your spring life into my shrivelled heart and bring greenness.

HELEN WILLIAMS

Perfect freedom

The Lord God commanded the man, 'You are free to eat from any tree in the garden; but you must not eat from the tree of the knowledge of good and evil, for when you eat from it you will certainly die.' (NIV)

'And into the forest I go, to lose my mind and find my soul,' wrote John Muir, a 19th-century environmentalist. As we enter the garden of Eden, in a clump of trees in the very centre, we see Eve do exactly the opposite – gain her 'mind' and lose her soul.

There is something significant about the trees called Life and the Knowledge of Good and Evil being at the centre of the garden – symbols of the life God himself has breathed and of the knowledge, or wisdom, that belongs only to him. People are not at the centre. His instruction to the man and woman not to eat from the second tree represents a boundary within which freedom existed – a moral boundary given for their good, a framework within which to thrive. God's service is 'perfect freedom', as the prayer reminds us.

God seems to be absent until he visits the couple later in the day. His intention had been that they should trust his word in his absence, but the serpent touches the woman at the point in her life where she was not ready to trust and to give everything over to her Maker.

Learning to trust God's instructions and promises, we know, is the way to true freedom, but how often we forget this! Reminding ourselves of and maybe writing down times we've seen God at work can help us to trust him for the future.

It's that basic trust, so vital to a child's healthy development, which is destroyed as the man and woman take things into their own hands. Suddenly, it becomes a world of division; union gives way to subordination, and there is shame about being made in the image of God. No wonder Jesus teaches us to pray, 'Lead us not into temptation.'

'Lead us not into temptation, but deliver us from evil.'

HELEN WILLIAMS

Jesus on the tree

He himself bore our sins in his body on the tree, that we might die to sin and live to righteousness. By his wounds you have been healed. For you were straying like sheep, but have now returned to the Shepherd and Overseer of your souls. (ESV)

We walk from the garden of Eden, where a tree has played a part in the undoing of the human race, into Jerusalem several millennia later. Here, trees permeate Holy Week. On Palm Sunday, branches are torn from trees and placed on the road for Jesus' entry into the city (Matthew 21:8). On Monday, Jesus curses a fig tree and by Tuesday it is dead (Mark 11:13–14, 20). On Thursday, Jesus refers to himself as the vine (John 15:1–5) and on Friday, as he walks to his death, Jesus says to the women flanking the road, 'If they do these things when the wood [or tree] is green, what will happen when it is dry?' (Luke 23:31). Peter takes up the story in Acts 10:39: 'They put him to death by hanging him on a tree.'

Not all translations use the word 'tree' for the cross, but it is a powerful metaphor for God's rescue plan and mission of 'mercy'. Jesus called us 'out of darkness', 'bore our sins in his body on the tree, so that we might die to sin', offers healing (remember Isaiah 55 last Wednesday?) and causes us to be born again to live in God's 'marvellous light' in the way he originally intended.

The theme of submission is so powerful here and challenges us to the core. We have an incessant drive to 'do it my way' as humans, and submission is often seen as weakness, cowardice and lack of conviction. Peter challenges the persecuted Christians, to whom he writes, to be internally secure and courageous, to set aside their personal agendas and to build relationships through respect and love.

Jesus' is the ultimate submission. Let us return to our Shepherd, to the one who cares, mends, treasures, leads, suffers and dies for us.

Perhaps you could bind two twigs with string to make a cross to focus on as you pray.

HELEN WILLIAMS

Trees in the desert

I will put in the wilderness the cedar, the acacia, the myrtle, and the olive. I will set in the desert the cypress, the plane and the pine together, that they may see and know, may consider and understand together, that the hand of the Lord has done this. (ESV)

Our walk has led us from winter to the promise of spring; from the tree that led to death to the tree that enabled life in all its fullness. Today, we think about what that new life looks like.

Until I visited the Holy Land, I had always imagined, naively, the Negev Desert as an area of endless sand dunes with the occasional oasis. It was therefore something of a shock to see mile upon mile of barren, rocky landscape. Travelling some years ago through this desert in a local taxi with my children, we were surprised when our driver suddenly stopped the car and motioned to us to get out. He poured a few drops of water out of a bottle on to the hard earth at the side of the road. Within minutes, small flowers started to push their way up – the desert was blooming!

God promises not just small flowers to his ransomed, restored people but that he will plant cedar, acacia, myrtle, olive, cypress, plane and pine in the wilderness. It's all down to water, of course, and the trees will flourish because of the rivers, fountains, springs and pools he promises. Once again, God might have just promised 'trees' for the renewed land, but we know he delights in variety!

If you are going through a dry or desert time at the moment, ask God for pools of his living water from which to drink (see Psalm 84:6–7). Ask for trees to grow from this season, for beauty to come from brokenness. Can you smell the pine, the cypress and the cedar? There is freshness as God sets about the restoration. Just to mention, though, often a desert time can be a preparation period for some particular ministry. Remember Moses, David, even Jesus.

'Their yearly trick of looking new is written down in the rings of grain,' Philip Larkin writes of trees. Lord, I want to be made new and ask for your living water. Thank you, though, for the 'rings' – the growing times.

HELEN WILLIAMS

Close encounters

Then the Lord said to Abraham, 'Why did Sarah laugh and say, "Will I really have a child, now that I am old?" Is anything too hard for the Lord?' (NIV)

'No two leaves are alike in a forest of thousands of trees; no two journeys along a familiar path are the same' (Paulo Coelho). Marvel at the diversity of God's creativity as, today, we follow six such journeys, stopping under various Bible trees.

We first stop at the great oaks of Mamre, a region of the leftover land Abraham graciously inherited, when Lot chose the more fertile land. The delightful encounter of Abraham and Sarah with the three heavenly visitors takes place under these oaks – a place of 'rest' and Bedouin hospitality. It's here that the 'very old' Sarah learns she is to bear a child!

In Judges 6:11–12, Gideon's divine visitor sits down to rest under the oak in Ophrah, before challenging the cowering Gideon to save his people from the Midianites: 'The Lord is with you, mighty warrior.'

An angelic encounter under a tree also faces the exhausted Elijah, as he flees from Jezebel in 1 Kings 19 and takes shelter under a broom tree. There an angel provides food and encouragement.

God grows a tree especially to shade Jonah (Jonah 4:6). When Jonah has more compassion for his little tree, attacked by a worm, than he does for the people of Nineveh, he suddenly begins to understand God's compassion.

The wood of the sycamore-fig, which Zacchaeus climbs in Luke 19:1–10 to see Jesus, was used to make coffins. Maybe the tree Jesus spies him in is a symbol of Zacchaeus 'dying' to his old life as he meets the One who brings life.

In our final arboreal encounter in John 1:45–48, we see Jesus meeting Nathanael and hailing him 'an Israelite in whom there is no deceit'. When asked by this sceptic how he knew him, Jesus answers: 'I saw you while you were still under the fig-tree.'

In each of these stories, trees are a place of rest or refuge. In the stillness of this space, God comes to challenge, to encourage, to restore or to transform. I would like to encounter you today, Lord.

HELEN WILLIAMS

The treasury of a good heart

By their fruit you will recognise them… Every good tree bears good fruit, but a bad tree bears bad fruit. A good tree cannot bear bad fruit, and a bad tree cannot bear good fruit. Every tree that does not bear good fruit is cut down and thrown into the fire. (NIV)

And so, as we near the end of our woodland walk, we come to the season 'of mists and mellow fruitfulness' or, if you prefer an exuberant children's hymn of praise: 'Autumn days when the grass is jewelled and the silk inside a chestnut shell' (HJS – 'Autumn Days'). My grown-up children still often break into this hymn at the top of their voices! There is so much to thank God for in the beauty of colour and the extravagance of fruit and harvest, although as I write from my home in the English countryside, I am grimly aware that this is not the story in so many places around the world. God's rules, even as far back as Deuteronomy 24, contain the instruction not to shake fruit-bearing trees twice, but to leave enough for 'foreigners, orphans and widows'. We must do much more to counter inequality.

Turning to Jesus' words recorded here in Matthew, Jesus uses trees (and wolves!) to speak powerfully about authenticity, warning his followers to watch out for wolves in sheep's clothing and to check out their 'fruit' before trusting them. In this context, it's a warning against false prophets, but it's a wake-up call to us too, to be known for bearing good fruit. I keep hearing and reading that authenticity is one of the things young people today prize most highly. I think they've had enough of spin, gloss, image management and empty promises. James takes up the same theme in his letter (3:3–18), suggesting how we might live authentically. It's worth a read, but especially notice the sentence in verse 17 saying that godly wisdom is always 'sincere'. Luke's version is also powerful and I particularly like this translation: 'A good person produces good things from the treasury of a good heart' (Luke 6:45, NLT). May that be me!

Autumn is fruitful, but, as leaves fall and plants die, it's also about letting go. Falling leaves become leaf mould which becomes soil in which new plants grow. May we let go of what's finished, in order to bring new life.
                                                                    HELEN WILLIAMS

Take of my fruit for others

On each side of the river stood the tree of life, bearing twelve crops of fruit, yielding its fruit every month. And the leaves of the tree are for the healing of the nations. (NIV)

We come today to the end of our walk among the trees of the Bible, and to the most vivid and exciting vision of a tree. The tree of life, planted in the centre of the garden of Eden, is now growing, in profusion, down both banks of a crystal-clear river. The very liquid of life is flowing from God's throne and through his city, and the tree is now the focus for complete wholeness – the 'healing of the nations', no less.

The tree of life is mentioned three times in Genesis and Revelation. The book of Proverbs also highlights four characteristics of this life, describing each as a 'tree of life': wisdom; righteousness; a soothing tongue; and a fulfilled dream.

The relationship between the tree in Eden and its counterpart in the New Jerusalem, too, is fascinating. They are both placed at the centre of their context, one in a garden, one in a city. The new tree produces fruit as in Eden, but a great extravagance of it – a crop every single month. As for accessing the tree, approaching it was banned in Genesis 3:24, whereas, in the heavenly city, the 'righteous' are now given open access to it. Like the fruit trees on either side of the river in Ezekiel's vision, the leaves of the new tree have healing properties and we assume that, like Ezekiel's, they 'will not wither, nor will their fruit fail' (Ezekiel 47:12).

I am reminded of the notice on the gate to the garden in C.S. Lewis' *The Magician's Nephew*, where the boy Digory picks the apple that will restore his sick mother. The note reads: 'Take of my fruit for others.' One thing is clear: the tree of life is not just for individuals. John's vision concerns the larger realities and transformation of societies, cultures and politics.

As we meditate on this astonishing vision of Eden restored; of old made new; of abundance rather than barrenness; of light instead of darkness; and of a way instead of a barrier, we pray for the healing of the nations.

HELEN WILLIAMS

The delight of Numbers

Rachel Turner writes:

If you have ever tried to read through the Bible cover to cover, Numbers is usually when you begin to fade. If you are like me, I breeze through Genesis and Exodus (there are some great stories in there) and then wade through Leviticus, being very impressed with myself for enduring those long chapters of laws. By the time I get to Numbers, I'm beginning to think, 'Ooo, I think this may be repeating itself a bit. I'll just skip ahead to Joshua, shall I? Pick up where the story gets good again.'

But Numbers has some wonderful gems in it. Little glimpses of God's heart, stories of brave and bold heroes, moments that make you smile and deep challenges for how to flourish in a season of dryness or pain. Numbers can be a wonderful book to explore.

For the next few weeks, we will be grazing through Numbers, stopping to pick up bits to sample and explore. Feel free to read the chapters between, or just skip along with the readings to take in Numbers, buffet-style.

But first, let me set the scene. Over the first few books of the Bible, we see God's creation of love broken by sin, separating people from God. We see the world descend into sin and depravity over and over, until only very few know God. We see him call Abraham into relationship with him, and promise to turn his family into a nation of people whom God will love, protect and bless. We see Abraham's family grow, and his great-grandchildren take refuge in Egypt during a famine, saved by God's divine plan using Joseph (his amazing technicolour dreamcoat left behind).

Four hundred years later, Abraham's family has grown into a nation of people, oppressed and enslaved in the Egypt that they once sought safety in. God sends Moses to speak for him to Egypt's ruler, Pharaoh, and God does mighty miracles, eventually resulting in his people being set free. God and Moses lead this nation of people, now called the Israelites, into the desert so God can teach them how to be in relationship with him, and fulfil the promise he made to Abraham. Numbers picks up one year into their time in the desert. Let us enjoy together what happens next.

The joy of counting

'From the whole community of Israel, record the names of all the warriors by their clans and families.' (NLT)

Fourteen months after the Israelites crossed the Red Sea, God told Moses to take a census, a recording of the names and numbers of the people. This command always baffled me. Since God knows all things, this census wasn't to gather information for God's use. I figured it had to do with Moses being able to create a military plan for the invasion of the promised land. But even that confused me because, repeatedly in scripture, we see God win battles with tiny armies or even no fighting at all. So why would he call for a census over a year into their time in the desert?

Have you ever noticed how real things become when we actually write them down? Taking account of something makes the situation starkly tangible. For fourteen months, the Israelites had lived in the desert, and yet their leadership didn't even know how many warriors they had, or who they were until God gently and firmly told them to count, and record names.

There are so many areas of life that we muddle through. Whether it's finances, a work project or a messy relationship situation, it can all feel like it is getting away from us. But God doesn't want that for us. He is the God who tells Moses to stop and take account of the reality in front of him, to truly face up to the exact situation they are in. Because once that happens, the next stage can begin.

After this counting, the Israelites were told their place to camp; they were given work assignments; they were ready to go. It took a moment of naming reality to prepare them to step into what was next for them.

God, you know every part of me, even the places I am not seeing. I want to move into what you have next for me.

RACHEL TURNER

Chosen by name

These are the names of the men who shall assist you: From Reuben, Elizur son of Shedeur. (NRSV)

If you are like me, as soon as you start to read this passage, a niggling desire rises within you to skip what you know is coming – the endless lists that make us feel like we are Year 1 readers. Hit the names 'Shemlumiel son of Zurishaddai' and you want to start flipping pages. You are not alone.

I actually love this list of names. I always smile at God's apparent micromanagement of a menial task. He felt it important to tell Moses exactly who he wanted to do the counting and recording. It can't have been that hard a job; surely anyone could have done it. But evidently God still wanted to pick the people, by name. I find that strangely comforting.

So much of our lives are mundane tasks that we feel anyone else could do just as well as we could. And yet, I believe that God has called us by name to do them. He has put great things in our hands, as well as everyday boring jobs, and yet he has given them to us to do. Not someone else. Us.

I love how God uses people's names all through the Bible. Each one had individual hopes and dreams for how their lives would turn out and then, out of nowhere, God chooses them. By name. How must they have felt?

It makes me ponder how begrudgingly I do the tasks that God has named me for. Whenever I read these names, it reminds me that God sees me, knows me and has called me by name to serve. And knowing that brings back a joy that I have often lost in the everyday.

Where have you been feeling unneeded or replaceable? Take a moment to share those feelings with God and ask him to refresh you to do the everyday jobs he has called you to do.

RACHEL TURNER

Camping with God

'The Israelites should make their camps around the Meeting Tent, but they should not camp too close to it. They should camp under their family flag and banners.' (NCV)

For 400 years, the Israelites lived in Egypt. The Egyptian religion dominated the architecture and culture of the cities and the towns they lived in. The Egyptians believed in many gods, each one having specific power and responsibility for something different. Ma'at was thought to be the goddess of truth, justice and harmony; Ra was the sun god; and Amun was the god in charge of the others and keeping the whole world on track. These gods had huge temples built for them, so people could come and beg for their favours. They were seen as aloof and distracted, changeable and distant.

For generations upon generations, the Israelites lived in this culture. And then the one true God rescued them from their pain and slavery, and brought them into the desert to teach them how to truly live with him. He didn't ask for a grand, huge, permanent temple, up on a hill. Instead, he asked to camp right in the middle of his people. There everyone could see him, at the heart of their community. There he could guide them, and speak with them. There he could move with them and constantly remind them of his love, provision and presence.

He wanted to move into the centre of this great mass of people because he loved them. I am so humbled that, even as faulty as I am, as chaotic as my life sometimes is, God still wants to be right at the centre of it. He doesn't want to stay far away, waiting for me to crawl to him. He wants to move into the centre of my life, to be with me, to be with each of us. Oh, how our days and nights would be different if we knew how close he truly is.

God, make me aware of how close you are camping in my life, that I may delight in the peace and joy of your closeness and companionship. Thank you for wanting to live among my mess.

RACHEL TURNER

Making amends

'When a man or woman does something wrong to another person, that is really sinning against the Lord… The person must fully pay for the wrong that has been done, adding one-fifth to it, and giving it to the person who was wronged.' (NCV)

A long time ago, I was so disengaged with my university classes that I got kicked out. I will never forget my main tutor's face when he told me how much he was personally hurt by my attitude, and how disappointed he was that I had chosen the path I had. Eventually, I reapplied to get back into university and, after a brutally honest conversation, my tutor chose to write a letter petitioning for me to get back in. He gave me grace, and I was overwhelmed with gratitude.

But as I was reading the Bible over the next few months, God kept bringing me back to this passage. I had sinned against God and this professor, and gratefully accepted the grace that was offered to me. But I never once thought that I should make amends. I realised that the Old Testament law gives us an insight into the heart of God for how to rebuild after damage has been done.

My tutor never asked for restitution; his grace had already been given. But I wanted to try.

I began to show up 20 minutes early to class to set up the room. I volunteered to be 'teacher assistant' in his classes, and assist any projects he needed researchers on: I would give him my time for free. I set out to try, in some way, to pay for the wrong that had been done.

As a result, the relationship, restored and built, turned into one of the greatest blessings of my life.

There is something about the process of making amends that serves to restore relationship in a way that merely accepting forgiveness does not. It doesn't come out of striving to achieve forgiveness, but rather to acknowledge the pain and damage caused and seek to minister to it.

God, thank you that you desire full restoration and justice in relationships. Is there any relationship where I need to make amends? Show me how to minister to people who I have hurt, that we may restore what was lost.

RACHEL TURNER

The awkward one

'So this is the teaching about jealousy. This is what to do when a woman does wrong and is unfaithful while she is married to her husband. It also should be done if the man gets jealous because he suspects his wife.' (NCV)

Okay, so let's just all take a moment to respond collectively to the reading by saying together: 'Arggghh!' I'll be honest. I wanted to skip this one altogether, but given that this is a passage that directly talks about women, I think we owe it to ourselves to wade into it. As a woman, I have a lot of emotions about this passage, and having struggled with infertility for over nine years, I have an extra twist of indignation about it. But if we step back for a moment, and consider the wider context, the glimmer of God's heart that is between the lines is something wonderful.

At this time, women had no rights. They were completely at the mercy of the men in their lives. Throughout God's law, he began to place rules down to protect women and give them access to justice. While this passage may sound bizarre, it actually established a structure of protection around women against false accusations. For a husband to accuse his wife, he had to bring a very expensive offering of barley flour. It would cost him to accuse her, so he would not do it on a whim. And rather than her being defenceless in a 'her word against his' scenario, the Lord himself said he would be her witness. While we in modern times may see all the inequality and injustice in this scenario, we should not lose sight of the safety that this regulation would have brought to Israelite women.

God repeatedly speaks throughout scripture of being a God of justice, who is a voice for the voiceless and protects the vulnerable. In the Israelite society, women needed a God of justice, and in this passage, we see him intervene with that heart.

God, there are so many women around the world in need of your intervention and protection. Bring them justice, change laws to protect them, and guard them now in their need.

RACHEL TURNER

The blessing

'The Lord bless you and keep you; the Lord make his face shine on you and be gracious to you; the Lord turn his face towards you and give you peace.' (NIV)

Every Sunday throughout my childhood, at the end of the service, our pastor would stretch out his hands and say this blessing over us. It was such a significant and important moment for me. As an adult, it still brings me to a stop.

For thousands of years, this blessing has been said over people, Jews and Christians alike. It is said because God himself told Moses that this was how Aaron and the priests were to bless people. God feels it so strongly that he wants, then and now, the leaders to repeat it over us so that we know he blesses us and keeps us; that his face turns towards us and shines on us; that he is gracious towards us and proactively gifts us with peace. What a wonderful God we serve.

I love watching children with their fathers, especially when children go through that phase where they are desperate to have their parents look at them. You can hear it across the room, 'Look Mum, look! Look at me, Dad!' Children naturally crave the face of their parents. They are desperate to have their full faces open and attentive just to them. I'm struck by how God's face is mentioned twice in this blessing, not just to give us his full face of attention and affection, but also his shining face of glory.

So often in life, we can feel out of view from a distant God. But when we hear this blessing, we are reminded that we have the full face of God the Father turned towards us. We don't need to compete for it or beg for it. It is his gift of love to his children.

Take a moment to reread the blessing slowly, three times. Highlight to God the aspect of the blessing that you are most grateful for in your life today.

RACHEL TURNER

Follow the leader

When the cloud moved from its place over the Tent, the Israelites moved, and wherever the cloud stopped, the Israelites camped. So the Israelites moved at the Lord's command, and they camped at his command. While the cloud stayed over the Tent, they remained camped. (NCV)

I hate moving. I really do. Right now, I am in the midst of packing up my house for yet another move, and I'm drowning in the admin of it all. We all face moves at some point: new jobs, new schools, new houses or new seasons of life. It can be agonising to try to figure out what is right; which move is God's plan or something to be prayed against; which move is to be embraced and which is to be resisted.

The Israelites were in a season of seemingly perpetual movement. God was training them in how to follow him. He was visible to them in a cloud, and every day they could see where he was and whether that meant they were to go or stay. If he was still, they stayed. If he moved, they followed. There were no guarantees of how long they would stay where they were, and no promises about the next place. The only thing they knew was that the God who loved them was guiding them and would be with them.

I naturally ask God so many questions when I am facing a move. Will we have friends, what will be our purpose, what do we need to change to live this season well, will my child be happy…? On and on the questions flow. When I read this passage, it reminds me that the same God who guided the Israelites is also guiding me. I may not see him in a cloud, but he is just as faithful to lead me and to be with me. My future is in his hands, and he sees it already. My job is to move and follow, ready for the next place that he brings me.

Now back to packing.

God, make me aware of your guiding, that I may follow you wherever you lead. Fill me with courage to walk away from the familiar into the next place you lead, with boldness and trust in you.

RACHEL TURNER

Linking arms

Moses said, 'Please do not leave us. You know where we should camp in the wilderness, and you can be our eyes. If you come with us, we will share with you whatever good things the Lord gives us.' (NIV)

Most movies or books about history take a grand event like a war, or a political struggle and help us understand it through the journey of a few characters or a family: *Braveheart*, *Schindler's List*, *Ben Hur*, *Beckett*. We see through a few characters' eyes the situation as a whole. In the Old Testament, we are often denied the small personal stories of family emotion and struggle that help us empathise with what it was like to live in those times. That's why I love this story. Plonked in the middle of a few chapters of grand description of how God moved people, and the regulations attached, is a wonderful little family moment between two brothers-in-law.

Moses' brother-in-law, who evidently has stayed with the Israelites, decides to leave, and Moses asks him not to.

Amid a group of people, all trying to re-establish what it means to be Israelites, a non-Jewish relative says he is going to go, and Moses pleads with him to stay. Moses tell him that his skills are needed and he is useful to them all. And he promises to share with him all the blessings that God is giving them.

In our efforts to become a church family, I wonder if we sometimes miss out on the power of linking arms with those outside that community and bringing them in, because we need them and value them and want to share with them God's blessing. Who outside our church families has skills and talents that we could use, even though they aren't fully a part of our Christian community? Who can we pull into relationship with us, and share God's blessing with?

Take a moment with God to think through friends and family who aren't part of your church community, but who you can invite to bring their skills and talents in, and who would be open to being blessed by him.

RACHEL TURNER

Honest prayer

Now the people complained about their hardships in the hearing of the Lord, and when he heard them his anger was aroused. (NIV)

The first time I read this passage, I remember it scaring me. The Israelites were complaining, and God heard their words and responded with consequences. I instantly clammed up in my prayer life with God, worried that I might accidentally anger him. There are so many people like me who come to prayer with this same fear, of praying wrongly or of not speaking well enough and feeling that God will respond in anger. But that isn't the God we see throughout the whole of scripture.

Jesus came to show us the heart of God as a beloved Father, a daddy. He chatted to God often in prayer, with a free flow of emotions and heart. David wrote psalms full of pain and frustration, of heartache and honesty in his relationship with God. The disciples chatted with Jesus, God on earth, with informality and imperfect understanding. I believe that our times with God in prayer are intended to be honest and gritty, informal and normal. So why was God angered by what the Israelites were doing?

This story isn't talking about people talking to God honestly, heart to heart. God loves that kind of relationship. This story is about a people who were complaining to each other about the blessings God had given them, and how they preferred life before relationship with God, before he rescued them and brought them to be with him. God gave them freedom, provided them with miraculous food, gave them his visual presence and guidance – and they were actively rejecting him.

Prayer is meant to be heart-poundingly honest, with nothing held back. We need not be worried that God will be angry when we share our worries or pain with him. He came to comfort us and love us through those things.

Take a moment to chat to God about things that cause you worry, pain or fear. Share what stresses you out, or makes you laugh. There is no right or wrong way to share your heart with God.

RACHEL TURNER

43

Tassels

Speak to the Israelites and tell them this: 'Tie several pieces of thread together and attach them to the corners of your clothes. Put a blue thread in each one of these tassels. Wear them from now on.' (NCV)

The first time I saw someone wearing these tassels, I was 14 years old and in a production of the musical *Fiddler on the Roof*. Several of the cast members were Jewish, and I saw dangling out from under their T-shirts four little ropes. They explained to me that because of this passage, they still wear a piece of clothing under their clothes that have these tassels on it to remind them of God's laws.

I was so struck by the practicality of having something tangible, to touch and see in everyday life, that sort of pokes at your heart and says, 'Remember God'. Throughout my life, I have tried to create for me what this might mean in my life, with varying levels of success.

When I got married, I bought a tree that I thought would live with me for a lifetime and be planted on my grave. I killed it with my very bad gardening skills within three months. Eventually, I found a pattern that worked for me. My laptop background is a constant reminder of what God is saying to me in this season of my life. One time, God reminded me of how he is like the ocean and it is my job to float in his love, so I found a picture of the ocean and put it as my screen background. Every time I open my computer, my mind and my heart are refocused on who God is.

God knows our hearts as humans. He knows that we need a tangible, constant reminder to keep our hearts and eyes focused on him. What would it be for you?

Take a few moments to spend with God, wondering with him what tangible action you can put into place that would constantly encourage your heart and mind to stay focused on him.

RACHEL TURNER

Who is in charge?

'I will choose one man whose walking stick will begin to grow leaves; in this way I will stop the Israelites from always complaining against you.' (NCV)

Have you ever felt that you constantly need to prove yourself? That you're constantly wrestling to maintain the authority you are supposed to have? Whether it's with your children, or at work, within a ministry, or within a place you volunteer, it can feel exhausting to face the barrage of challenges and criticism that we often receive.

Moses and Aaron felt the same way. Over and over, significant Israelites complained about their leadership, thought that they should be replaced and criticised how they were leading. The opposition was vocal and harsh, and sometimes it became almost a physical challenge.

But when those challenges came, it wasn't Moses or Aaron who stood up and enforced their position of power. They never once instigated a showdown, or flung their credentials in the face of their opponents. When others challenged how they were leading, or even whether they should be leading at all, Moses and Aaron took a step back and watched God handle it. God is the one who chose them to be in the position they were, and they trusted God to keep them there if that was what he wanted. In this story, God made it clear by causing Aaron's stick to miraculously blossom. In other times of challenge, God made much more drastic interventions, but it was always God who stepped in.

It can be so discouraging when those whom we lead pick away at our leadership. Their criticism can be crushing and cause us to doubt ourselves. We can easily feel the need to defend ourselves and fight to maintain our position. But if God has put us in that place of authority, then he also is faithful to defend his choice. He is working on our behalf; you can count on it.

God, help me let go of my need to fight for position and power. I trust you to place me where you want me, and support and defend me in the roles you have called me to.

RACHEL TURNER

A comedy of errors

'When you sent messengers to me, I told them, "Balak could give me his palace filled with silver and gold, but I still cannot go against the Lord's commands. I could not do anything, good or bad, on my own, but I must say what the Lord says."' (NCV)

This is one of those long stories that spans several chapters, and this chapter comes at the end of it. After the Israelites have camped in the desert with God, God begins to lead them into encounters with tribes and communities who live in the outskirts of the new land. No one is too pleased to see a huge swarm of Israelites coming towards them and so battles break out between the Israelites and various tribes.

One local king decides to hire a prophet to come and curse the Israelites. Fortunately for the latter, God has other plans, and every time Balaam the prophet positions himself to speak, God has him bless the Israelites instead of cursing them. The poor king, Balak, grows increasingly frustrated as three times his chosen prophet blesses instead of curses his newfound enemy, the Israelites.

The blessings that God gives Balaam to speak are wonderful. They speak of his love for the Israelites and how strong he is making them. They speak of his commitment to them, and the future he has for them. And in the middle of it all, God gives some clues to the coming of Jesus. We might hear these words around Christmas, 'A star will come out of Jacob; a sceptre will rise out of Israel' (v. 17, NIV). The star that the wise men followed, the prophesy that they knew, came out of this comedy of errors when one king tried to manipulate a prophet to curse God's people and it didn't work.

Paul tells us in Romans 8:28 that 'in everything God works for the good of those who love him' (NCV). I am so encouraged by this story because I see in it the glory of a God who can take an enemy's plan and turn it to such beautiful good.

God, thank you that no evil plan can stand in your way. Thank you that you can turn all things for good and that even now you are speaking blessings over me.

RACHEL TURNER

A girl called Noah

They went to the entrance of the Meeting Tent and stood before Moses, Eleazar the priest, the leaders, and all the people. They said, 'Our father died in the desert.' (NCV)

These five sisters are some of the bravest women we get to hear about in the Bible. In a society where women had very little power, they chose to do something extraordinary. According to the law, inheritance passed from men to men, from a father to a son. If there was no son to inherit, then it passed from that family to a relative. When their father died, it appeared that their portion of the coming promised land would be denied to them. They wouldn't get to have a portion of it for themselves; that was the law.

So, they chose to challenge it. Not quietly, not casually. They approached the Tent of Meeting where God's presence was, and stood before 'Moses, Eleazar the priest, the leaders, and all the people'. I love to imagine what that must have been like. How small and insignificant they might have felt. How scared they might have been, knowing how God had responded to other people who had seemingly challenged Moses and Aaron. How passionate they must have been, to want for themselves the fulfilment of a land in which to live and flourish. In front of the most powerful leaders in their society and the vast sea of their community, they stood and demanded a portion of God's promise. What astonishing bravery. What courage and grit!

And what happened? God changed the law. God himself put women into the chain of inheritance forever because five women were bold enough to ask for it. I love how God responded so quickly and so decisively in their favour, as if he was eager to give them what they asked for.

What injustices exist in our world that are just waiting for us to step up and demand a change?

God, make us bold to speak against injustice, whether for ourselves or for others. Use us to bring change that lasts for all other generations to come.

RACHEL TURNER

Commissioning a new leader

'Take Joshua son of Nun, a man in whom is the spirit of leadership, and lay your hand on him. Have him stand before Eleazar the priest and the entire assembly and commission him in their presence.' (NIV)

The music thundered at the end of the service as she looked in my eyes and said, 'I'd like to pray for you and officially pass on the mantle of leadership that God gave me for this role.' When I was told I would be taking over this leader's national role, I felt that beautiful combination of terror and excitement. I had worked for several churches at this point and had had many 'commissioning' services where a congregation prayed for me at the start of my job, but this was something different. This was a moment where the person who had been doing the job before me deliberately laid her hands on me and prayed for me and my leadership in front of others that I would be leading. As she prayed, I was overwhelmed with such power and peace. It was unlike anything I had ever experienced before. When I moved on from that role, I made sure I did the same for the leader who came after me.

There is something so significant about blessing those who take over from us. Whether it is a volunteer role or an employed one, whether it is as a parent blessing our children as they become parents themselves or whether it is handing on our ministry to someone else, commissioning those following us is powerful. There is something God honours in the deliberate and public passing on of authority and responsibility. There is something that happens inside us when we either give that commissioning, or receive it.

In God's kingdom, as we raise up leaders, let us not forget to commission them with grace and power as they step into their roles. And let us be humble enough to ask for it as we step into new roles ourselves!

Take a moment with God to think about anyone that you still need to commission into their new role, even if they have been in it for a while.

RACHEL TURNER

Overwhelmed: anxiety, fear and insecurity

Ann Warren writes:

The world we live in today seems to be in absolute turmoil. I wonder if there has ever been a time when things have seemed quite so uncertain and so likely to erupt into chaos.

With volatile, unpredictable leaders around the globe, and the UK going through enormous upheaval which seems likely to bring about huge change, is there not every reason to be fearful or anxious about what the future holds?

Terrorists threaten our everyday lives, apparently certain of their belief in a god who turns children into suicide bombers and demands the destruction of anyone with different religious views. Meanwhile, rumours abound of end-time prophecies coming to pass.

At such times, it is helpful to remember that in many ways this kind of life is not so very different from the New Testament world that the early Christians knew. Here was no safe Christian comfort zone, but a frightening time when any one of the believers might be captured, crucified or thrown to the lions.

And yet, they lived and died with amazing faith and trust in the God they had come to know in the person of Jesus Christ, who had lived and worked among them. Knowing him personally was the key to their unswerving faith.

Those who followed Jesus during his earthly ministry walked with or listened to Jesus in person. They knew him just as you know your friends and colleagues – and they trusted him enough to suffer and die for him if need be. The Jesus they knew personally was worthy of this love and trust, and they knew that whatever happened they were safe in his care and the future he promised. We can know Jesus personally today too.

Trusting in God's care for you

Humble yourselves, therefore, under God's mighty hand, that he may lift you up in due time. Cast all your anxiety on him because he cares for you. (NIV)

If you have grown up in a loving, caring family where your parents really looked after and protected you, then you may find it easy to trust in this promise that God cares for you.

But what happens if you do not have this experience and you have only been used or hurt by those whose job it was to look after you?

For many years, I had no experience of the secure feeling that most people naturally grow up with. Trusting in God, or in anyone for that matter, seemed a completely unnatural thing to do. I was orphaned at seven and adopted by a couple whose marriage was already on the rocks, disintegrating some 18 months later amid all the hurt and bitterness that often accompanies divorce – not exactly the ideal foundation for trust or faith of any kind!

But only a few weeks ago, I came across a verse which, although I must have read it many times before, suddenly highlighted for me what had brought about change and enabled me to trust for the very first time.

I heard afresh those wonderful Christmas verses from John's gospel: 'The true light that gives light to everyone was coming into the world… He came to that which was his own, but his own did not receive him. Yet to all who did receive him, to those who believed in his name, he gave the right to become *children of God* – children born not of natural descent, nor of human decision or a husband's will, but born of God' (John 1:9, 11–13). Somehow, God had reached out to me in the darkness and enabled me to 'cast all my anxiety on him because he cared for me' – even if no one else did.

Is there anything in your past experience that is blocking your belief in a God who cares for you? Take time to think about this and bring it to the Lord in prayer – and if necessary ask a trusted Christian friend for help with this.

ANN WARREN

Don't let fear take over in your life

For the Spirit God gave us does not make us timid, but gives us power, love and self-discipline. (NIV)

Fear is paralysing. It grips us by the throat and prevents us from doing and saying the things we would like to say – or that we know deep down we should.

Most likely, this fear started a long time ago in childhood, when we were bullied or made to fear speaking up or admitting what we really felt. Unfortunately, until we deal with this, it will often come back to haunt us with thoughts such as 'You know you can't do that', or 'Who do you think you are?'

I wonder if Timothy had some deep-seated insecurities which led to Paul challenging him, encouraging him to 'be strong in the grace that is in Christ Jesus' (2 Timothy 2:1) and reminding him that God's Spirit 'does not make us timid' (v. 7).

The thing about childhood fears is that they can still seem as enormous to us as they felt at the time. But if, now, we face up to these childhood fears in the power of God, they will no longer have the same power over us.

Years later, when I finally found the courage to stand up to a woman who had terrorised me as a child, I was amazed to discover how easily she apologised and backed down!

Fear can also choke the expression of love because, in the grip of fear, we may only be thinking about how we come across, instead of lovingly considering the needs of the person we are talking to. If we are released from fear, we can talk about our own Christian experiences in a relaxed and natural way without being afraid of what others may think.

Are there times when you feel frightened to speak up naturally about your faith? Spend some time praying about what might be behind this, and ask God to help you deal with whatever fear you are experiencing.

ANN WARREN

No fear in love

There is no fear in love. But perfect love drives out fear, because fear has to do with punishment. The one who fears is not made perfect in love. (NIV)

Sadly, there are people who have learned to think about God in terms of the punishment that he will one day deal out for sin. Brought up as a Roman Catholic, I and my fellows were urged regularly to go to confession in case we should die in a state of mortal sin and be sent straight to hell or purgatory when we died. Not surprisingly, fear of judgement loomed very large in my early thoughts about God.

We heard no mention at that time of the amazing grace of a God who loved us so much that he sent his only Son to die for us and pay the penalty for our sins. When I finally understood this for myself, it provided the most wonderful release, opening the doors to a genuine faith in a loving God who would be there for me whenever I called out to him.

Unfortunately, the stick rather than the carrot has often been seen as the correct way to bring up children, with the view that they will only do the right thing out of fear of punishment. I have to admit that at times, when my own children were driving me crazy, there seemed to be something to be said for this approach…!

However, anything more than a session on the 'naughty step' does very little to enhance parents' relationships with their children. So much more can be achieved by spending time helping them to understand our love and concern for them – so that they will actually *want* to do what we ask of them. It is the same in our relationship with our loving Father God.

Are there still ways in which you fear God and his punishment, or have you understood his great love for you? Maybe memories of childhood or some other unhelpful experience? Talk to God about them.

ANN WARREN

Don't let worries take over

Therefore do not worry about tomorrow, for tomorrow will worry about itself. Each day has enough trouble of its own. (NIV)

Once you allow yourself to get into the habit of worrying, there will be no end to it: one worry will just lead on to another.

As the verse above tells us, new worries are likely to present themselves every day, whether in the newspapers or in our own personal lives – and these can overwhelm us. The only answer is to bring fears and worries immediately to God, asking him to carry the burden – and then leave them there.

Like most people, I have found this very difficult to do – probably because of all the terrible things that happened to me as a child. But in my prayer diary, I have kept a record of faithful answers to prayer, so that I can refer back to these in times of real trouble.

Many years ago, my first husband was asked to take over and run a group of plantations in Papua New Guinea, some 12,000 miles away. On arrival, we discovered massive problems, and also a very hostile director threatening redundancy unless Peter could improve things in an impossibly short time. We knew very few people in the country and no one whom we could trust to ask for advice or support, but still we prayed that somehow God would help us.

To our amazement, about half an hour later the doorbell rang and there at the door was a woman I hardly knew, but recognised just enough to know she was a fellow Christian. 'Is there anything I can do to help?' she asked in a rather embarrassed way. 'I was praying and I suddenly got a very clear sense that you needed me.' This extraordinary answer to prayer eventually led to a complete change in the terrible management situation, and a wonderful boost to our faith.

Are you facing seemingly impossible problems at the moment? Try stepping out in faith to ask God to help you and take the worry off your shoulders.

ANN WARREN

Do not be anxious

Do not be anxious about anything, but in every situation, by prayer and petition, with thanksgiving, present your requests to God. And the peace of God, which transcends all understanding, will guard your hearts and your minds in Christ Jesus. (NIV)

When something terrible seems about to happen, it may feel totally impossible not to feel anxious! How do we know that God will help us cope with our financial situation? Can we really trust him with the bullying problem at school?

The minute things start to go wrong in our lives, our bodies will probably start tensing up, causing both our anxiety and our blood pressure to soar. This is known as the 'fight-or-flight response', intended to protect us when there really is a need to escape from danger. Simply committing this situation to God and looking for his peace at such times can feel so completely counterintuitive.

Inevitably, bad things will happen to us. We live in a fallen world and this place is not our ultimate home. The promise is not about keeping us away from trouble, but about how God will help us to cope when we are in the thick of trouble. The only way to learn this is by actually going through the eye of the storm and discovering for ourselves the amazing peace that he has promised us.

Without doubt, the most traumatic time for me was when my first husband was dying of cancer. Having lived through such an unhappy childhood, I really could not imagine how I would be able to cope with the terrible experience of Peter's death. But, impossible as it seemed, the peace of God was there for me during that time, together with a powerful sense of his loving presence in the many friends who surrounded me. His peace really did transcend all understanding, and guarded my heart and mind at a time when I so desperately needed it.

What problems are lurking on your horizon? Can you put aside the anxiety and, instead, trust in the peace of God to guard your heart?

ANN WARREN

Worry achieves nothing

Therefore I tell you, do not worry about your life, what you will eat; or about your body, what you will wear… Who of you by worrying can add a single hour to your life? Since you cannot do this very little thing, why do you worry about the rest? (NIV)

When things go wrong in life, worry can appear to be the most natural course of action. It's as if we feel we have got to 'do' something! Our minds will frantically search for ideas to solve the problem, or ways round it, becoming more and more ragged with each new stressful thought.

As these verses graphically point out, if we can't even add a single hour to our lives by worrying, how on earth do we imagine that worry can solve anything?

In yesterday's passage from Philippians, we were told to present our requests to God by prayer and petition with thanksgiving, so that he would grant us his peace. But in order to have this peace, we must leave the problem with him and not snatch it back again. There is a big sign over God's 'worry pond' that says, 'No fishing here!'

I have found that God often deals with my problems in ways I could not possibly have dreamt up myself. His resources are endless and well beyond my very limited imagination, so I am gradually learning not to try to deal with problems in my own strength!

Sometimes coping with a worrying situation is all part of the learning process intended to help us grow in maturity and trust God more. He is not some kind of indulgent daddy who will immediately rush to our rescue, and often we need to learn to survive with his help living *through* troubles rather than be rescued *from* them – hard as that may seem at the time.

I have learned far more from living through the difficult times and overcoming them with his help than I would ever have learned in the easy, calm passages of life.

Heavenly Father, help me to trust you when I hit difficult times in my life and not to worry. Please give me the strength to overcome these with your help.
                                                                ANN WARREN

God is in control

Do not be afraid. I am the First and the Last. I am the Living One; I was dead and now look, I am alive for ever and ever! And I hold the keys of death and Hades. (NIV)

One of the hardest things to cope with is the feeling that no one is really in control of world events. Deep uncertainty like this can remove all sense of security and is a fertile breeding ground for fear.

Political crises everywhere, leaders hurling threats at one another, desperate imaginings of what might happen next on the world stage. Learning to trust God when newspaper headlines seem so overwhelming and frightening is no easy task.

But this passage reminds us that, ultimately, God is still in control, as the first and the last, and he holds the keys to what happens in the future.

When I first became a Christian, I naively assumed that God would always look after and protect me so that nothing bad would ever happen to me again. But I had completely missed out on or ignored the fact that I had also been called to take up my cross and follow him.

We all need to learn to trust God through the difficult times and to grow stronger in our faith. Christians in many other countries are really being tested in this way. But we were never promised an easy option. 'You will hear of wars and rumours of wars,' Jesus tells us in Matthew's gospel. 'But see to it that you are not troubled. Such things must happen but the end is still to come' (Matthew 24:6).

People are frightened about world events, and they need to see that we trust our God for the future. We have to be able to say with confidence that we believe God is still in control, no matter how terrible things may seem. Above all, we need to learn to trust him completely with the future ourselves.

Heavenly Father, please help me to trust you with the future as trouble increases on the world stage, and show me how to daily grow stronger in my faith.

ANN WARREN

Living in relationship: Ephesians

Tania Vaughan writes:

There are times in life when we may forget who we are and what we are doing. As the pressures of the world we live in press in on us, it can be hard to lean into God. Whenever I, or someone I know, is feeling disconnected from God or is uncertain about God's calling, this is the part of the Bible I always head to. The letter from Paul to the church at Ephesus covers the core aspects of our Christian life and journey.

Split into two halves, Paul's letter encourages us in our identity; it is balm to the heart that is feeling unloved, a confirmation for those feeling unsure and a reminder for those whose self-esteem is low. The first half shows us who God is, and reminds us of his abundant grace and of what he has done for us through the death and resurrection of Jesus. These first three chapters help us reconnect with why God has chosen us and what he has called us to.

The second half of the letter offers disciples an overview of how to live in relationships as a community of people obedient to God. It tells us that life will not be easy but, by applying the truths of the first three chapters and giving us the right tools, Paul shows us how it is possible to stand firm. This letter is the place I go to when my faith wobbles, when I forget who I am or what I am doing. It brings me right back to God and sets me back on the right path. It confirms me in my identity as a child of God and gives me the courage and direction to be able to live out my faith.

During these next two weeks, I want to offer this letter to you as an encouragement for you in your identity, your calling, your community and your discipleship journey.

To be known

For he chose us in him before the creation of the world to be holy and blameless in his sight. (NIV)

There is something in me that wants to be known, to be liked and to have relationships. However, I also don't want to be truly known. People know what I want them to know about me. My life is hidden behind carefully crafted images on social media. My heart is guarded by a fixed smile and a mumbling of 'I'm fine' in a crowd of semi-strangers. There are few, very few, people in my life who really know me and, even then, there is always more that they don't know. There is nothing wrong in that; in fact, it is appropriate. We cannot open up our lives so the whole world can see everything, but sometimes that can make us feel a little lost and lonely. But all this that we keep to ourselves, hide from view or shy away from, is known by God.

There is nothing to fear from him knowing every hidden corner of your life. He has known you since before the creation of time and it was then that he chose you, even if you haven't yet chosen him. You were not chosen because of your perfect life or for what you can accomplish; you were chosen simply because you are you. Knowing you, all of you, does not disappoint God. In truth, he takes pleasure and delight in you as his child.

God does not know you by what you choose to show him; he does not view your social media profile and see only what you choose to share. God sees you through the perfect life of Jesus Christ. You have been chosen to be holy and blameless in his sight. That is the 'you' God sees and that is the woman he knows.

Think about what you may still be trying to keep from God. Take time to bring it before him and ask him to shine light into those areas.

TANIA VAUGHAN

To know

And God raised us up with Christ and seated us with him in the heavenly realms in Christ Jesus, in order that in the coming ages he might show the incomparable riches of his grace, expressed in his kindness to us in Christ Jesus. (NIV)

When I moved across the border from England to Wales, I left behind a lot of friends and had to begin the journey of getting to know new people. I met people in different contexts and got to know them at different levels of friendship. I still don't know anyone very well, not like the friends I'd spent years getting to know; it takes time for people to open up.

God isn't like that; he wants us to know him completely. He reveals himself fully to us through Jesus. He does not give to us bit by tiny bit, but instead lavishes us with love and grace. God wants to be known. He created humankind to live in relationship with him, not just as virtual friends but as his children. God gave us his Son so that, through him, we could see, know and relate to God himself.

It takes time to know God, not because he has not revealed himself fully in Jesus, but because we need the time to understand and know him. Through Jesus and his word, God reveals his character, his purpose and his great love for us – but we can only receive from him gradually. If we tried to take it all in one go, it would surely overwhelm us. So he walks a journey with us, allowing us to get to know him at our pace.

It is tempting to think we know him – we've read our Bibles for years and walked a well-trodden path – but there is still more to know. There are incomparable riches and grace for our lives that we have not yet seen – but they are there to be found.

What do you need to do to renew your commitment to taking time to get to know more of God and start receiving more of his love and grace?

TANIA VAUGHAN

Living in community

So then you are no longer strangers and aliens, but you are fellow citizens with the saints and members of the household of God. (ESV)

I am an introvert: I like time on my own and I like quiet. My husband is the opposite and loves to be around a lot of people and noise. For his 40th birthday, I threw a huge surprise party which he loved. My 40th was very different, with a few friends and a quiet meal. Even though I am happy with my own company, I cannot be a disciple alone. We were created to be in community; even silent-order monks live together. Over the years, I have learned with my husband to enjoy the company of others and he has learned to enjoy quiet nights in with a book.

Although I do not need people around me, I do still crave a sense of belonging. I have a need to feel a part of something and to be included.

As believers, we have become fellow citizens with God's people, no longer excluded as foreigners. A community of believers is the only place where you will get people from such diverse walks of life coming together. It is not just your immediate community that you are now a part of, but a community that stretches all around the world. Community in Christ is bigger than we can see or even know, and we are together as one body.

In Jesus, you and I are joined together with believers across the world as members of one massive household. As an introvert, that thought should scare me but in fact it amazes me: I am no longer a stranger to you or to a sister on the other side of the world. We are part of something much bigger and more wonderful than we can understand.

Pray for a Christian person or project in a different part of the world, remembering that they are part of your community.

TANIA VAUGHAN

Sharing the good news

His intent was that now, through the church, the manifold wisdom of God should be made known to the rulers and authorities in the heavenly realms, according to his eternal purpose that he accomplished in Christ Jesus our Lord. (NIV)

I have been a member of a national slimming club for years and I love sharing with the group the tips and recipes that have been good for me. Losing weight changed my life and I wanted to share that joy with others.

Losing weight has not changed my life anywhere near as much as Jesus has, and yet I find it much harder to share that joy. There are no recipes for success and there is no plan to follow that is easy to relate and yet I do want others to know how God has changed my life.

The good news of God's lavish goodness to us is not for keeping to ourselves; it is a gift to be shared. God gives us the life changes, the stories and the grace to tell others. As well as our own life stories, there is plenty to share from the gospels. It can be hard to relate those stories in a way that seems relevant today, but the more we know them the easier it is to do.

I have recipes now that I can cook without even looking at the book, because I know them so well. I could tell you how to cook without looking anything up, and I may even put my own twist on it. This is the way in which we are called to know God's story and his word, so that we can share it with confidence and without needing to look everything up every time. When we know something well, we can add our own personal 'twist' and tell it our own way.

What do you need to do to know God's word so well you can share it with confidence? Join a Bible study group? Read a deeper study on a book of the Bible? Pray about it now.

TANIA VAUGHAN

Serving together

I… urge you to walk in a manner worthy of the calling to which you have been called, with all humility and gentleness, with patience, bearing with one another in love, eager to maintain the unity of the Spirit in the bond of peace. (ESV)

The community we belong to is one that Paul encourages us to live in with peace and unity. This far-flung, worldwide community of believers is a huge body of people, and it is also the smaller communities that we meet with regularly. Being part of a community is more than showing up each week. Community is a place where a diverse range of people come together to serve one another in humility and with patience.

We may not always recognise the importance of being involved in our communities and we can get into a habit of just turning up to a group or meeting, taking what we need and leaving again. We can feel too tired, too busy or, like me, too introverted, to want to get involved. However, worshipping together, serving one another and studying God's word in community help us in our own journey and they allow us to be a blessing to others.

My son is at university and, when he comes home, it takes a while for him to remember that he is no longer in a student house just looking after himself. Here, he needs to get involved in the day-to-day business of a home and family. Our family is much more united when we work together, especially with the household chores!

Paul calls us to live a life worthy of our calling by living in unity and being eager to maintain it. In order to show humility, love and patience to one another, we need to be involved together. We cannot be community alone and it is only when each member of the body does their part that real unity can be realised.

Think about the community groups you are part of – Bible study, church, etc. Are you an active member of the whole body or do you just turn up? How does it help you in your journey?

TANIA VAUGHAN

Discipleship

The gifts he gave were that some would be apostles, some prophets, some evangelists, some pastors and teachers, to equip the saints for the work of ministry, for building up the body of Christ. (NRSV)

A young girl I know is learning a martial art and, when she achieved her third grading, she began teaching the children below her, alongside the experienced teacher. She was not an expert and was still learning, but she could share what she had already learned with those who had less experience. She used what little she knew and helped to prepare others for their next grading.

As disciples of Jesus, we are on a journey of learning to live for him. Each of us is gifted in different ways to enable us to help others. We do not need to know it all or be experts in living for Jesus in order to share what we know. We are called to share our journey with others and what we are learning along the way: you can use the little you know to help prepare others for their next step.

In reading these verses, we may think that because Paul mentions very specific roles that nurture God's people, they don't apply to us; after all, we are not all pastors or prophets. It is true that some are called to very specific roles, but we are all called to testify to what God has done in our lives to encourage others. Remember Legion, the possessed man Jesus restored to full health (Mark 5:1–20)? Jesus said to Legion: 'Go home to your friends, and tell them how much the Lord has done for you.'

As I share my thoughts here to encourage you on your journey, I am also being encouraged by others who are on a different part of the journey from me.

Every disciple of Jesus is commissioned to go and make disciples and to use what they have learned to teach others about Jesus.

Read Matthew 28:16–20 and think about one person who is younger than you in age or faith whom you could come alongside to share your experience of knowing Jesus and help them on their journey.

TANIA VAUGHAN

Using our gifts

From him the whole body, joined and held together by every supporting ligament, grows and builds itself up in love, as each part does its work. (NIV)

As an introvert, I do not do well in a noisy room and children are not my favourite age group. Serving in children's church would not benefit either the children or me! I think by the end I would be hiding under a table from the noise. I know I can teach God's word and I love doing it, but I also know I can't teach in children's church; I am not gifted in that way.

However, I love the Tuesday afternoon ladies club, where at least one person nods off but no one runs around screaming and banging drums. Just because I can teach God's word does not mean I should teach everyone. My personality and my gifting have a particular resting point that God uses to build up that part of the community.

Each one of us is gifted in different ways: it may not be to teach children, but you might love them and be able to handle a room full of them. Maybe you are gifted in service and love making coffee. Perhaps you are diligent in prayer for those in your community. Are you great at paperwork and keeping everything organised?

You are a part of the body and are needed for it to function as one body. Each part must do its own work and not just what needs doing. Too often, people are serving in an area they are not gifted in because there is a need. This can lead to frustration and the body not functioning well; it can also stop someone gifted in that area being able to use their gifting. Each skill and every passion is a gift from God which, when used for the good of the community, builds it up.

What are your specific gifts and passion? If you aren't sure, ask God to show you. Are you using them wisely?

TANIA VAUGHAN

Be someone different

You were taught to put away your former way of life, your old self, corrupt and deluded by its lusts, and to be renewed in the spirit of your minds, and to clothe yourselves with the new self, created according to the likeness of God in true righteousness and holiness. (NRSV)

As we grow in the way we know God, exercise our gifts and live in community, people around us may notice we are living differently. Unintentionally, we are changing because of the way we are intentionally trying to live out our faith. Paul talks about putting away our old self and taking on the new, which comes with a new attitude that starts in our minds. As we live together in unity and serve one another using our God-given gifts, we take on a new way of living.

As the community of believers in an 'alien' world, there are things we need to be careful about. Living in a world where the accepted values are so different from God's can desensitise us to what is true and good, and we can find ourselves acting in ways dishonouring to God. Here, Paul lists the snares of this world that we need to avoid. It is hard sometimes not to feel told off by his list of 'don'ts'.

However, rather than feeling discouraged because we cannot stop our negative behaviours in one go, let Paul encourage us with advice as to how our attitudes can gradually change. He advises those with an anger problem not to 'let the sun go down on your anger' (v. 26). What a difference that would make! He tells those who engage in 'evil talk' (including gossip?) to choose words that bring encouragement so that negativity is replaced with positivity. He tells those prone to taking what's not theirs to do something useful with their hands for the benefit of others. This is not a list of don'ts but a reminder of the changes we can make to stand out as different in our world.

'Be kind to one another' (v. 32). That's a good start!

Read the passage again and, rather than focusing on the things we may do wrong, make a note of the positive changes Paul calls us to take.

TANIA VAUGHAN

Living in obedience

Let no one deceive you with empty words, for because of these things the wrath of God comes on those who are disobedient. Therefore do not be associated with them. (NRSV)

Have you ever tried walking the wrong way on an escalator? It's hard work but, with a bit of effort, it can be done. But why would you? It's so much easier to take the escalator the right way and it certainly avoids those bemused, sidelong glances because you're going the wrong way!

But what about when God asks us to take a stand, to live differently? When we choose to live in obedience to God, we can often feel like we're taking the escalator one way while everyone else is going the other way. We are called not to be influenced by those who are disobedient to God's word. People will tell us that something is not that bad; everyone does it and surely God won't mind; you're not hurting anyone.

Making a stand for God can leave us feeling unpopular or isolated. It can also feel a little pointless or unnecessary if we are not making a stand that is big and dramatic, such as the civil rights activist Rosa Parks, who stood (or rather sat!) against racial prejudice. However, even a small stand for God can be powerful. When you walk away from the gossip over the tea break or speak kind words instead of fuelling it, people will soon see that you are someone who is kind and trustworthy. In sexual matters, there will be Christian women who take a stand against sleeping with a boyfriend before marriage, despite it being culturally acceptable. Again, in a world that is consumed by possession and money, Christians will look for opportunities to give money away.

Dare to be different! You're not asked to change the whole world, but you may want to rock your own corner of it.

Pray with an open mind and ask God to show you where he wants you to take a stand in your life.

TANIA VAUGHAN

Unintentional discipleship

Be careful then how you live, not as unwise people but as wise. (NRSV)

When we looked at discipleship a few days ago, we thought about how we can share our own discipleship journey and the ways in which we have grown. However, the effect of our discipleship on others is not always intentional; sometimes we can impact others without even knowing it.

There have been various adverts over the years against smoking and abuse, showing the impact of adults' behaviour on children who then seek to imitate them. This is not behaviour learned through teaching but through watching.

In the same way, we are not aware of the people who are watching us and taking notice of how we live. If we want to be the good news of Jesus, we must imitate him in the way he loved and gave himself up for us.

We can only imitate someone we know well, and this comes back to knowing God and understanding what his will is, not just for our lives but for the world he created. We can do this by acknowledging that all good things come from him and living a life of thankfulness for everything we have.

Paul calls us 'children of light' (5:8), recognising that the light comes from the goodness and truth of knowing God. It is this light that we shine when we imitate God. We are able to show those who watch us, sometimes from a distance, that the love of God is real. We do this when we forgive as he has forgiven us and love in a way that is beyond measure, the way that he loves us.

Pray that God would direct the way you live and keep you attentive to those around you, that you may impact them for Jesus.

TANIA VAUGHAN

Submitting to God

Submit to one another out of reverence for Christ. (NIV)

This is one of the most difficult passages for women to read and hear, especially because of the way in which it has been interpreted and abused over the years. However, once I took time to really understand it, it became one of my favourite passages. Understanding it comes from starting at verse 21 and not verse 22: there were no verses and no breaks in the original text. Submission is an act of obedience, not to another person but to God. Submission is not a power struggle, it is not a show of weakness and it is not letting the other person win. Submission is acted out of reverence to Christ and it is mutual.

As a wife, I still struggle with the word 'submit' but, when I view it as a loving act as described in these passages, I can ask, 'How can I love my husband in obedience to Christ?' I know that he also asks, 'How can I love my wife in the way that Christ loves?' When the answers are lived out in obedience to God, it is submission.

Submission is an act of love. Paul calls it a 'profound mystery' (v. 32) as he compares the loving act of submission to the way in which Christ loves the church. As we seek to live as Christ lived, we struggle in many ways to love as he did, whether that is loving our enemies, taking time for those who are different from us, or mutually submitting to one another. These acts of love are where we witness to the abundant and profoundly mysterious love of God towards his people.

If you struggle with this passage, I encourage you to find a good book or commentary and take time to study it more fully.

TANIA VAUGHAN

Preparing for the hard task ahead

Therefore put on the full armour of God, so that when the day of evil comes, you may be able to stand your ground, and after you have done everything, to stand. (NIV)

Whether facing an exam or planning to bake a cake, there is a certain amount of preparation required. Revision is needed or ingredients bought, pencils are sharpened and recipes are learned. The time of this event is coming and you need to be prepared for it. I know it sounds a bit dramatic for baking a cake and maybe you're wondering why I would put such an everyday task under a heading that speaks of a 'hard' task. Well, for me it is; baking is not my strong point. In fact, I never bake and it was the scariest task needing preparation that I could think of.

If I approached the day of cake-baking without having read through the recipe a number of times and double checked the cupboard for ingredients, I would be ill-prepared for the task.

Paul says we need to put on God's armour 'so that when the day of evil comes' (v. 13), we will be able to stand. He doesn't say that we need to prepare *in case* that 'day of evil' comes, but for *when* it does. There is no doubt that days of testing will come and we need to be prepared for them. We may not even recognise at first when the 'day of evil' is upon us, so it is essential to be ready. Every day, we need to put on 'the full armour of God' that will protect us every step of the way.

Preparation for 'the day' or days requires us to read and reread the word of God to ensure we know how to live and how to stand. And we need to be constant in prayer and worship. We have to check the store cupboard of our heart and soul to ensure they are full of the good things of God. Then we will be ready to stand and withstand anything the enemy may throw at us.

As we spend these last few days in this same passage, ask God to prepare you for what you may face in the future.

TANIA VAUGHAN

Learning to recognise the enemy

For our struggle is not against flesh and blood, but against the rulers, against the authorities, against the powers of this dark world and against the spiritual forces of evil in the heavenly realms. (NIV)

As we saw yesterday, not only do we need to be constantly ready for spiritual battle, but we need to recognise the enemy who is against us. Paul says our struggle is against the powers of this dark world and spiritual forces in the heavenly realm. Our preparation is for a spiritual enemy that we can neither see nor hear coming. Peter says this enemy prowls like a lion looking to devour (1 Peter 5:8). How do we stand against an enemy we cannot see?

Paul lists seven tools God gives us to discern this enemy and protect ourselves. This armour is familiar, but how often do we take the time to ensure we are wearing it properly? Paul says we need to: 1) know the truth of God, 2) live in the clothing of righteousness that Jesus gave to us, 3) be ready in our knowledge of the gospel and its message, 4) be strong in our faith, 5) be secure in our salvation, 6) be confident in the word of God and 7) pray in the power of the Spirit.

It is in this full armour that we are able to stand. We would normally expect to put on armour to go into battle but Paul tells us that, with God's armour, 'you may be able to withstand on that evil day... [and] to stand firm' (v. 13, NRSV). The NIV says 'stand your ground'. We need to remember that the armour is for protection, not for battle. The battle belongs to God and he fights for us. In the same way as he did for the Israelites, 'the Lord will fight for you, and you have only to keep still' (Exodus 14:14, NRSV).

I regularly find it helpful to pray through these verses every day for a week at a time. Why not try it for yourself?

TANIA VAUGHAN

Praying in power

Pray in the Spirit at all times in every prayer and supplication. To that end keep alert and always persevere in supplication for all the saints. (NRSV)

A rowing boat without an oar is at the mercy of the water. That water may be a still pond and the boat becomes stranded in the middle, unable to move and going nowhere. Or that water could be a fast-flowing river and the boat is taken along without direction, at breakneck speed and sometimes heading for a waterfall.

A boat without an oar is, for me, a picture of a life without prayer in the power of the Holy Spirit. Prayer keeps us alert to the leading of God: it is the tool of discernment that allows us to see the advancing enemy. Jesus has given us his Spirit within us to enable us to pray in power, to hear God and to discern his voice over all others. A life without prayer can keep us stuck in one place where we don't hear God's leading or we become complacent in our faith.

For me, if I go without prayer for any length of time, my life ends up on a flooded river out of control, running faster than I can keep up with and in a direction I'm not sure God has called me to take. The enemy schemes to pull us away from our time with God and to keep us stuck in one place; he aims to take control of our lives, to lead us in the wrong direction. Without the power of prayer in the Holy Spirit, we may not even realise we are no longer in control.

A prayerful life through the Holy Spirit keeps us alert and focused for the spiritual battles on our journey. Prayer wraps the armour of God around us and keeps it there.

Consider ways in which you could make prayer a more regular and more powerful part of your discipleship journey.

TANIA VAUGHAN

Prayer songs

Victoria Byrne writes:

Written communications can leave a long legacy. I heard yesterday of some eleventh-century Japanese love letters published recently. I'm curious to read the thoughts of someone living so long ago. But that's not so long compared to the psalms, which were written at various times between about 2,500 and 3,000 years ago. In the next few days, we will study a personal selection from books 2 and 3 (these books comprise Psalm 42 to Psalm 89). They are beautifully written, using references from nature and human experience that are familiar to us still. Here, we find expression for our own cries of joy and delight; betrayal and confusion; and everything in between. In sharing how they make me thoughtful about my own life, I hope they will help you pour your heart out to God.

Do read the whole psalm given, and not just the excerpt. A psalm's power often lies in the emotional journey described between the first word and the last. Psalms encapsulate the dynamic spiritual life of poetic, creative people, whose emotional truth is vivid and relevant to any believer. The authors are varied; while some are famous beyond these pages (for instance, King David and his son King Solomon), others have left nothing in the public record but these few stunning jewels.

They have been used as the songbook of worshippers for millennia. Often, they include encouragement or directions to sing, clap, praise God and turn to him. The authors share personal challenges and react to convulsions of national politics and change. They direct us to recognise the presence of a faithful God who is willing and able to rescue. Through these psalms, we sing to each other: 'Come and see what the Lord has done.' We find models of grief and sorrow; thanksgiving; rededication to God; psalms for the public square and private reflection. As the temple singers would have sung them to the people and each other, let's join in with our sisters and brothers across space and time in calling each other to engage with God.

Humans have been experiencing the same emotions for thousands of years, and we get to read some of their thoughts beautifully expressed in poetic language. Here, we find out what brings them pain, joy and hope. These are our prayer songs.

Hope

Why must I go about mourning, oppressed by the enemy? Send me your light and your faithful care, let them lead me; let them bring me to your holy mountain, to the place where you dwell. (NIV)

The psalmist prays that God's light (revelation) and faithful care will lead him into God's presence, away from dejection and hopelessness. By contrast, when I'm feeling dejected, I've already lost sight of God. However, if I've got as far as acknowledging a positive attribute of my heavenly Father, I'm already halfway to finding a fresh approach. I love the way the psalmist identifies the qualities of God which will give him hope, even when he's not feeling hopeful. It's as if he's throwing a pebble attached to string across to the other side of a chasm, to which he can attach a thick string of greater confidence, and finally a rope, until there's something bridging the gap that will carry his weight.

It's too easy to make a little less effort, and become stuck in a vicious circle of worries or impossibilities: 'I can't do this, so that's going to be impossible, and then it will all go wrong.' There's always another way. As we read this psalmist's thoughts, our hope rises with him. Psalms are wonderful for reframing the way we are thinking about our own situation. If we pause and check our assumptions, we may find that God is trying to show us another view.

If you'll allow me a prosaic example: when our cooker hood broke, I encountered a series of technical mysteries that made fixing it seem impossible. A couple of times, the right way forward appeared wrong, so I didn't pursue what would in fact have helped. Much later, when I stopped letting negative assumptions trip me up, I gained a fresh sense of perspective and fixed it quickly.

When a situation seems hopeless, God has a way (1 Corinthians 13:7): the question isn't whether he wants to help us, but how.

God has 'light and faithful care' to offer you today: what do you want to talk to him about?

VICTORIA BYRNE

Finding the river

There is a river whose streams make glad the city of God, the holy place where the Most High dwells. God is within her, she will not fall; God will help her at break of day. Nations are in uproar, kingdoms fall; he lifts his voice, the earth melts. (NIV)

Verse 10 is likely familiar to you: 'Be still, and know that I am God', using that phrase God called himself when speaking to Moses (see Exodus 3:14; often translated, 'I am who I am').

'Be still' is a command to stop struggling so that God can make you aware of his presence, which will keep you safe. I'm reminded of a toddler so full of energy that you can't get their coat on. I'll forever remember this psalm as the one God surprised me with on the morning of the European Referendum result in 2016.

The rest of the psalm describes scenes of war and vengeance that seem at odds with the way this verse is often quoted, or printed reassuringly on everyday items! In the course of carefree times, we might take God's presence lightly. There are other days when the shock and shift of life's surprises give this psalm a powerfully fresh relevance.

Yesterday, I heard of the sudden death, from a heart attack, of a wonderful church leader, a colleague in the church, the husband of a special lady with whom I feel a particular connection. He was someone who had an open heart towards others: his loss is already being greatly felt. In such painful moments, we realise how fleeting life is. After acknowledging the tragedy and pain, I'm also aware of this rising battle cry in me, with a fresh realisation that the battle is real: seeking God's presence and perspective is vital.

Today, in reading that command, 'Be still,' I hear him saying, 'Stop struggling in fear, I know the enemy. He's powerful, and you're in pain, but I'm bigger: I have overcome him, I will exact justice, be at peace.'

'We don't need a theology of intimacy with the Lord: we need to actually be intimate with him' (Jeremy Riddle, speaking at David's Tent, UK, 2016).

VICTORIA BYRNE

Praise God, the source of every blessing

He chose our inheritance for us, the pride of Jacob, whom he loved. God has ascended amid shouts of joy, the Lord amid the sounding of trumpets. (NIV)

Today, passing a garden wall, I noticed lying on the bricks the beautiful rosehips and crab apples which had fallen in abundance from the trees above. It was a tiny picture of God's grace. There are so many blessings in my life which have been freely granted: for example, I have been blessed to be born in a country that respects the rule of law, that has universal healthcare, where the weather and the wildlife are not usually life-threatening. But maybe, lately, I haven't consciously considered these and other blessings that fall on my life.

I've noticed that I'm writing in my spiritual journal a lot less recently. That practice was a helpful way to untangle confusion and to listen for God's words for me in uncertain times. Recently, life has been full of happy activity, creativity and joy, and I've journalled less. Perhaps my journalling was rather lopsided: only working on problems, not appreciating the joys and blessings.

I love the way the psalms cover the full breadth of our emotions and experience of God, and give us a balanced diet. If you are numb, or confused, or unspeakably happy, or you don't even know what you are, you can read through psalms until you find an echo of your own heart. In this way, the psalms help us engage with our emotions. As we acknowledge our feelings to God, we enlarge our heart for what's going on in or around us. Whereas I used to journal mostly in difficult seasons, the writers of the psalms acknowledge the bad *and* the good times, and the emotions that go with them. Reading this psalm, I found my current sense of exhilaration reflected in these verses full of emotional, euphoric words. That prompted me to thank God for my own blessings.

For further reflection, read Deuteronomy 8:10–14.

VICTORIA BYRNE

Share the happy news

We will tell the next generation the praiseworthy deeds of the Lord, his power, and the wonders he has done… Then they would put their trust in God. (NIV)

Three months ago, my friend and I spent a week away seeking God's plans for our futures. We prayed and listened. My ideas ranged across travel, creativity, food and writing, but it all felt like wishful thinking. Back home, I decided to pray again with another friend. And then I discovered she was looking for someone like me to help her write about an Indian community for a cookbook! We travel there for six weeks to do the research, and that's how this is shaping up to be a really exciting season.

Until yesterday, I thought I'd done a good job of making all this happen by myself. Then I discovered notes I made while seeking God's will. I found he'd given me lots of clear pictures which had shaped my subconscious expectations, so that when the opportunity arrived, it felt right. The project combined everything I loved. It would, however, take courage, and God had been giving me messages for a year about bravery. Suddenly, I could see the craftsmanship of God's plan, how wonderfully he had brought things together, and I'm in awe. Bravery is easy when God is so clearly in charge.

When I joined our church, I feasted on autobiographies from the library: people having adventures with God. I discovered he was faithful and exciting. Let's feed on everyone's accounts of their experiences with God. He hasn't changed. The Bible is a storehouse of God's victories in people's lives. He is the same God who loves you. If you keep a journal, reread it sometimes. If you know older Christians, ask them. If you know younger people, tell them. He is not finished with you.

Remember today whose child you are: your father is the King of hope; so set your crown on straight, and look forward.

VICTORIA BYRNE

Let it go

Create in me a pure heart, O God, and renew a steadfast spirit within me. Do not cast me from your presence or take your Holy Spirit from me. Restore to me the joy of your salvation and grant me a willing spirit, to sustain me. (NIV)

Shame is a destructive state to be in. I remember seriously messing up the venue arrangements for a large rehearsal. We all trooped to an alternative venue, miraculously available minutes away, but my every step was heavy. It was easily fixed, but at the time I felt so ashamed… and at the same time grateful for being forgiven by colleagues. I sat next to someone I didn't usually find it easy to chat to, yet in his friendly words he clearly overlooked my mistake and still seemed to trust me, which calmed me.

When we sin, we usually harm others. When forgiveness is withheld in any direction, it risks dividing us. Verse 4 here must be a rhetorical statement; after all, he has sinned against at least two people, but it's as if he's saying: 'However bad my sin, more important to me is that I've endangered our relationship.' God's covenant with King David (and the country) is what matters to David most.

This psalm is David's response to the realisation that he's guilty of a great crime. What's extraordinary is that he remains secure in God's covenant. We see that he trusts that God hasn't already banished him from his presence. He's not begging to be allowed back into God's presence: he knows he's never left it. This is central to David's relationship with God. He never stops trusting that God is listening. We could follow his example in remembering that God is with us ALWAYS, because he has promised that and he keeps his promises. He speaks reconciliation over us as he invites us into repentance.

'Surely your goodness and love will follow me all the days of my life' (Psalm 23:6).

VICTORIA BYRNE

God's love in response to distress

If an enemy were insulting me, I could endure it… but it is you, a man like myself, my companion, my close friend… I cry out in distress, and [God] hears my voice. (NIV)

David is mourning what used to be a close friendship. He is pained by the memory of two good relationships gone bad: he remembers the unity of spirit he had with his son Absalom – now in rebellion against him – as well as his formerly trusted counsellor Ahithophel, who has conspired with Absalom against him (see 2 Samuel 17). David's desire to run away to the desert suggests he would go anywhere to get away from this situation – the desert is not an easy place to be.

Weeks ago, someone I trusted was arrogantly rude to me, and I reacted very badly, so much so that I felt I'd put them in the right and me in the wrong, but I still felt aggrieved. I poured out my anger to God and eventually received God's patient love. Then I could untangle what had happened, forgive my friend and repent for my part. God's love untangled the confusion and freed me. It came from the opportunity to acknowledge to God my messy feelings.

Any attack is painful, but when it comes from someone we trust, it can be intensely painful and confusing. The mixture of fear, indignation and self-doubt that results is difficult to handle. In David's honest words, we see him troubled by several things: the fear of threats, the anger at betrayal, the desire to avenge and yet mourning the sweet fellowship he experienced with those same people. Finally, he changes his focus and reminds himself that God, who will have his way, is the opposite: a constant friend, a rescuer, full of justice and ultimately in charge. As we read of the friend's broken covenant (v. 20), God reminds us of his covenant with David, and how it was fulfilled in Jesus.

For further reading, take a look at 1 Peter 5:6–10 in which Peter (who disowned Jesus on the night of the arrest) quotes verse 22 from today's psalm.

VICTORIA BYRNE

Singing hope in the darkness

I cry out to God Most High, to God, who vindicates me. He sends from heaven and saves me, rebuking those who hotly pursue me – God sends forth his love and his faithfulness. (NIV)

As a student, I stayed at a youth hostel in Verona where I met a girl who talked about the highs and lows of travelling: when she was anxious, she would sing to overcome her fear. That struck me as impressive self-management. She's come back to mind often over the years when I've been anxious or been otherwise stuck in various mindsets.

This psalm is possibly two compositions melded together; it certainly has a change of pace at verse 5. It reminds us that God is bigger than our problems and is eager to run to our rescue. Sometimes it's hard to believe he thinks well of us, especially if we are disappointed with ourselves or we have been beset by troubles, and we can begin to think he is angry with us. But his love never fails. Jesus' love didn't stop when his disciples let him down. When we take a step of faith and trust that he loves us, trust that we've heard him, we discover his promises are true.

God has been speaking to me for years now in terms of 'singing'. I'm learning that when God the Holy Spirit speaks to me using images of songbirds, he's speaking about freedom, communicating his good news or simply reminding me to be joyful. We each carry a song. I heard someone say recently: 'A bird doesn't sing to waken the dawn; it sings because dawn is coming.' It sings because of a sure hope.

God promises a sure hope to the world through the Bible and his people. When we intentionally let God into our lives, we are open to his healing, reconciliation, peace, joy and the list goes on. His hope is real.

If you feel like you're in the bottom of a pit today, look up. What do you see? Talk to God about it. Or maybe sing?

VICTORIA BYRNE

Wanting to see justice done

They say, 'Who will see it?' They plot injustice and say, 'We have devised a perfect plan!' Surely the human mind and heart are cunning… The righteous will rejoice in the Lord and take refuge in him. (NIV)

Apparently, the secret to acting or writing believable evil characters is to understand how the baddies are heroes in their own eyes. Any of us can have self-deceptive moments, but some people seem to live that way permanently. They believe that what they want is right and pursue it without regard for the well-being of others.

I know people who have been on the receiving end of long-term, hurtful behaviours where someone has acted in irrational and destructive ways while blithely ignoring the hurt they're causing.

Within wider society, our daily newspapers are full of people who seem to get away with damaging and evil behaviours. Knowing that there are people around who choose to hurt others for their own selfish gains can be deeply troubling for those of us who try to live by God's values. How do we respond? Do we retreat to a safe place and disengage from the world?

David finds the answer to the evildoer's rhetorical question 'Who will see it?' and enlightens us in verse 7 onwards. God knows, and he will see justice done.

In the Lord's Prayer, when Jesus tells us to forgive others, he also reminds us that we ourselves do wrong. Only God can be trusted to be perfect, and to bring about perfect justice.

When I am treated unjustly or I read of greater injustice in society, I find it comforting to know that the truth will come out eventually. In the final lines of the psalm, David tells himself to rejoice in the Lord and not obsess about what bad people are getting away with. I don't mean we should avoid seeking justice, especially for others, but we can have peace that God sees everything; he is just and his truth will prevail.

Lord God, thank you that you are a just God who loves mercy.

VICTORIA BYRNE

Looking back, looking forward

For you have been my hope, Sovereign Lord, my confidence since my youth. From birth I have relied on you; you brought me forth from my mother's womb. I will ever praise you. (NIV)

The roots of the word 'confidence' mean 'with faith'. This psalm got me thinking today about the 'headlines' of my life. When I was young, I was not confident in most situations. I went to church and was quite religious, but I thought there was perfection and satisfaction to be achieved in doing everything right, for example in singing beautiful choral music together. I was unaware that God had much more to offer: that he was real enough to want to have a personal relationship with me. It's taken me a few years to admit to myself that that was how I saw things. I guess there was some pride in the identity I made for myself then, but it was a perfectionist's vision that could only lead to disappointment whenever things weren't exactly right.

When I look back, I'm grateful that God has made me happier and wiser than I was as a teenager. I see now that confidence is not based in my achievements, but in my worth to him. In hindsight, I can see that God wanted to protect me from the stress of my perfectionism – but I was not really listening well enough to hear his loving, fatherly words. With his confidence in me, the holes in the road are not so deep and success is less perilous. His is the steadying hand.

I don't need to compare my spiritual journey with other people's: it's better to focus on how far he's brought me, as does the psalmist. This psalmist recalls how God was good to him before, and trusts him for the future. It's a life's journey to know God and respond. God doesn't change. Even if I can't see the way forward, I know that God can: he's out in front.

For further reflection, read Psalm 139.

VICTORIA BYRNE

You are influential

Endow the king with your justice, O God, the royal son with your righteousness. May he judge your people in righteousness, your afflicted ones with justice. May the mountains bring prosperity to the people, the hills the fruit of righteousness. (NIV)

I find it fascinating to read the private thoughts of a successful leader. Those business transformation stories, or autobiographies of former political leaders, always draw me in with their revelations of, and reflections on, what it is like to lead a big company or even a country.

When we read autobiographies, we are invited into the often complicated lives behind the public face. When I watch the news, I sometimes think, 'I'm glad it's not me waking up and remembering I'm running the country,' and that reminds me to pray for our leaders. Leaders have to make the difficult decisions: the rest of us often sit back and can make up our mind after the event!

In the opening verse of this psalm, we hear the private thoughts of King Solomon, who was famously wise. As he took on the mantle of leadership, his prayer request was for wisdom. His priorities in leadership feature in the very first verse of this psalm. Solomon is praying for blessing *in order that he can be a blessing*. He wants to bless people by improving conditions for the poor; he wants power in order to lift up the weak. He has quite a specific agenda.

This psalm is a leader's prayer for himself, but it is also a prayer for all of us to use. We are all influencers, even if we don't lead a nation. Every one of us has influence in our immediate circle. Even if you are someone who through illness or immobility lives physically cut off from others, you can pray to our heavenly Father, the King of kings, and so, little by little, your prayer influence can change the world.

Solomon knew what he needed from God to equip him as a leader. Do we pray about our leadership and influence?

Ask God how he sees your influence.

VICTORIA BYRNE

Fighting for us

You are radiant with light, more majestic than mountains rich with game… At your rebuke, God of Jacob, both horse and chariot lie still. It is you alone who are to be feared. (NIV)

I confess, I often read psalms about God's wrath rather hastily. I do believe he is the judge and will have the last word, but I'm still recovering from my childhood bias that saw God's judging my every move. As an adult, I am working towards a more balanced view. I find this a helpful illustration: God is like a judge who privately writes a cheque to cover the huge fine he has correctly imposed on his guilty but repentant friend.

Making instant judgements has never been more popular. We are encouraged, especially through social media, to declare instantly formed likes, to take sides on controversial issues, to approve or condemn. Sometimes the pressure to 'judge' seems overwhelming. Which calls to action should I as a Christian respond to? How do I 'judge' each controversial issue? It's not our responsibility to take all the burden of judgement on ourselves. That's the responsibility of the 'Judge of all the earth'. We are only responsible for what God sends us to do according to our prayerful understanding, tested in community with others.

I know God judges me but I also know he loves me, inspires me, lives in me and forgives me. He offers mercy and forgiveness when I repent; his self-sacrifice sets me free from the consequences of my sin. God's judgement and his offer of forgiveness and renewal apply to every person he has made.

This psalm also reveals God's judgement anger burning when he sees the enemy attack his people. As we engage daily in the spiritual battle that is 'not against flesh and blood', we can safely leave judgement to our God who is magnificently victorious over all evil.

'This is the confidence we have in approaching God: that if we ask anything according to his will, he hears us' (1 John 5:14, NIV).

VICTORIA BYRNE

We can trust him

The Mighty One, God, the Lord, speaks and summons the earth from the rising of the sun to where it sets. (NIV)

Last month, I travelled to India (see 6 March). A friend and I hoped to find great recipes and stories so that we could write our fundraising cookbook. There were so many unknowns about that trip. Yet God had already shown us in extraordinary and ordinary ways that he wanted this to happen. We knew he could make it work, but we didn't know what difficulties we would have to overcome. Each time we prayed we received reassurance, but we were heading off into a real adventure.

As we took off into the starry London sky, I knew that God could see the countries we would be flying over. I was excited to think that we would be coming back with heads and hearts full of interesting memories of people and food, and I had so many questions.

As we landed the following morning, we were taken to meet our first contacts. This was the first sign that it would all go well. We were able to watch someone cook straight away, and we saw that God was going to exceed all our hopes. Right in front of us, she cooked a very familiar spicy lentil dish, which just happened to be my favourite. God knew exactly how to reassure me! I'd travelled thousands of miles, but he was able to make me feel right at home.

God is magnificent. The world is his. He doesn't need us to use our cleverness to second-guess him. He just wants us to show up and partner with him as he builds his kingdom on earth. When we look to him for provision, guidance and purpose, we can be sure that he is the 'parent', the one with the responsibility and the resources. When he calls, he provides.

Lord, thank you that you are a big God who is all-powerful and has plans for me. Help me expand my horizons to match yours. Help me to pray big prayers.

VICTORIA BYRNE

Hearts set on pilgrimage

Blessed are those whose strength is in you, whose hearts are set on pilgrimage. As they pass through the Valley of Baka, they make it a place of springs. (NIV)

When we are intentional about living for God, he weaves our lives together into a fabric that's shot through with purpose. That is not always easy to see at the time, but it's still true. We frequently do not see the pattern of what God's making out of the mess, any more than a loom's shuttle going back and forth can see the design. But as we persevere, we may discover that God has been able to make something beautiful out of difficulties and even messes.

Some seasons are just horrible. When we hear of something terrible, our thoughts do not instinctively turn to gladness that God can make something lovely out of it. But as we go through difficulty, we do experience valuable things that are rarely learned in easier times. For example, we discover the liveliness of God's word in our present experience. The Valley of Baka is not easy to traverse; it's a place of tears. But God can hold our hands through the worst situation, and when we get to the end of that valley, we will find that he has gifted us something very precious along the way.

Once, years ago, I suffered unfair accusations from someone I had to see regularly. Friends supported me through that time and their kindness and care was an immense blessing. It was good to know I had friends who were ready to pause their busy days and be kind to me. Their response still makes me feel secure now, even though the crisis has long passed. It's the same with our relationship with God: when we have known his closeness during hardship, we carry that intimacy into happier times.

What did you learn about God during a difficult season?

VICTORIA BYRNE

Connections

You who seek God, may your hearts live! The Lord hears the needy and does not despise his captive people. (NIV)

This morning, I prayed for strength to face the day ahead. This psalm is written by David and echoes many themes of books 2 and 3 of Psalms. Here is reliance on God despite hellish suffering. David stays faithful and even clings to God more strongly when challenged. We see the despair expressed as he describes events and emotions, but David always seeks refuge in God. Here is the familiar move towards praise, determination to appreciate God's goodness. Even if he cannot see it now, he declares his sure expectation that he will be full of joy later (v. 30); it becomes an ode to God's faithfulness. We read the promise of rescue for God's people and of defeat for those set against him.

Which verses stand out for you? These psalms are a prism through which God's light shines on our own lives and problems. Sometimes the situation described in the psalm is so dire, and ours is not, that we might feel disconnected. But every time I read a psalm, I have a chance to examine my own life through its filters. I'm facing hard work with new challenges, while still needing perseverance with the existing ones.

Unlike David here, I'm happy at this time, but as I study this psalm, I realise his feelings echo those of some of the people I work with, or am about to work with. God's word compels me to confront the reality of how some people are feeling: they are the 'neighbours' God puts in my path. I need to take care of the ones who might echo David's words. And right there, I realise God has already answered my prayer of this morning, that he would ready me to return to work after my holiday, equipped and ready to care.

Which verse or idea from the psalms still resonates with you from these two weeks?

VICTORIA BYRNE

The life of Joseph

Chine McDonald writes:

The story of Joseph is one of those biblical accounts that I am most familiar with. When I think about Joseph, son of Jacob, I think of early memories of Sunday school textbook illustrations of his amazing coloured coat. I remember dramatic enactments of the story during church services. As a fan of musicals, I will also never forget watching Andrew Lloyd Webber and Tim Rice's production of *Joseph and the Amazing Technicolor Dreamcoat* at the London Palladium. This was the first musical I saw live and remains one I can recite all of the words to. Even as a young child watching the show, I remember thinking how rich the story was – full of colours and characters. This famous account of Joseph's life has everything you need in a good story: twists and turns, goodies and baddies, character development, family betrayal, politics, sexual temptation, tragedy, humour and faith.

But this is more than a story. Joseph's life teaches us so much about what it is to be placed in positions of authority. It teaches us the importance of humility and integrity, no matter the situations in which we are placed. It teaches us that God has a plan – not just for our individual lives but for whole people groups. It is amazing that the seemingly insignificant events of Joseph's early life would ultimately lead to a change in the course of the history of Israel.

Through the life of Joseph, we see also that nothing can thwart the plans of God, even though at times it might seem as if God and those we love have abandoned or forsaken us. As you read these notes over the next two weeks, I pray that this very familiar story will speak to you in new ways.

My prayer is also that you will be reminded afresh of the awesomeness of the God we serve and know that no matter the situation in which you currently find yourself – whether you are doing amazingly well or struggling – that situations can change. God is right there with you in the midst of it: Immanuel.

We are all God's favourites

Now Israel loved Joseph more than any of his other sons, because he had been born to him in his old age; and he made an ornate robe for him. (NIV)

Some people just seem to have all the luck. There are those for whom everything seems to go right. These lucky people float through life, with the right doors opening for them at the right times – the best job opportunities, the right relationships, the perfect children and the perfect home.

At times, it can seem like God has favourites, people written into a winning story, while others are left flailing through life despite their devotion to God. Maybe you've never experienced the green-eyed monster rearing its head in your life. But if this is something you recognise, then you might understand the feelings that Joseph's brothers experienced in relation to their brother, the wonder kid, the apple of their father's eye. We are told in today's passage that Jacob loved Joseph more than any of his other sons. They were jealous of his standing in his father's eyes. And we probably know what this jealousy leads them to: secretly selling their brother into slavery.

I wonder how the twists and turns of the Joseph story would have panned out differently if Jacob's sons had felt secure in the love that their father had for them rather than focusing on their father's favouritism towards Joseph, exemplified in the ornate robe that he had been given. As children of God, each of us must recognise that, despite our position, despite all that we have done and all that we haven't – whether we have it all together or not – God loves each of us equally. He has no favourites. Or better still, every one of us is his favourite! What a difference it would make if we grasped just how much he loves us.

Bring to mind one person whom you have envied. Pray for God's blessing upon them, and pray that God might reveal his love for you in new and profound ways.

CHINE MCDONALD

Holding on to your dreams

Joseph had a dream, and when he told it to his brothers they hated him even more. (NIV)

Joseph is perhaps the most famous dreamer in history. But Martin Luther King Jr comes a close second. This civil rights activist hero of mine gave his most famous speech during the march on Washington in August 1963. To thousands and subsequently to millions, he spoke about his dream that one day the barriers between races in the US might be broken down. Sadly, he was killed before his dream was ever realised. And the world is still waiting.

Joseph too had dreams. His dreams told him that God had big plans for his life and that eventually he would rise to more prominent heights than his father. It must have been difficult for him to hold on to those dreams in those moments of his life when he was betrayed or imprisoned. Perhaps he felt that the dreams God had given him were never actually supposed to come true.

Have you ever had a dream you believe God has given you? Have you had prophetic words spoken over your life? Have you seen those dreams come to pass, or are you still waiting? I know that in my own life, I have been at times excited by the dreams God has given me, the call he has placed upon my life or the things he has said will come to pass. But sometimes, the trials and disappointments of life – or even just mundane day-to-day living – can drown out the voice of God and make you doubt that you had ever heard him correctly in the first place. The story of Joseph reminds us that, no matter how long it might take, our God-given dreams really can come true.

Lord, please give me a waiting and expectant heart that you will fulfil in me all you desire for me.

CHINE MCDONALD

God's purpose through flawed characters

Then he had another dream, and he told it to his brothers. 'Listen,' he said, 'I had another dream, and this time the sun and moon and eleven stars were bowing down to me.' (NIV)

It's probably true to say that, when Joseph was a young man, he lacked humility and emotional intelligence. The early toe-curling encounters with his brothers, in which he tells them of the dreams he had had, implying his superiority and foretelling that they would all bow down to him, display his arrogance and/or his naivety. Anyone who has siblings knows of the complicated dynamics and rivalries that go on within families; but any sibling who voices a sense that they are in any way better than the others is likely to stoke intense feelings among their brothers and sisters.

Joseph – like all of the Bible's heroes – is not perfect: Moses was a murderer, Noah had a drink problem and David was an adulterer. And yet we know that in each of these cases, including Joseph's, God's will came to pass. Despite the flawed way in which Joseph made his dreams known to his brothers, they did come true. His family, as we see later on in the Genesis story, did bow down to him.

What this shows us is that God can use every one of us to accomplish his purposes. He alone reigns supreme so that none of us can boast that anything was all our doing. We also learn, from stories like Joseph's and those of other flawed biblical characters, of God's transforming power. God is able to make all things new and that includes us. He does not leave us as we are, but takes us on a lifelong journey of transformation. This is the power of the gospel – Jesus, the only perfect one, comes to seek and save us, bringing total renewal and transformation.

If an account were to be written of your life and included in the Bible, what would your 'flaw' or 'flaws' be? Pray that God will take you on a journey of transformation to be more like him.

CHINE MCDONALD

Watch your words

When he told his father as well as his brothers, his father rebuked him and said, 'What is this dream you had? Will your mother and I and your brothers actually come and bow down to the ground before you?' (NIV)

The rise of social media has meant that our words are captured in the ether forever. Increasingly, those in public life are being pulled up for comments they made on their social media accounts years before. People today expect an almost impossible standard from those in public life. People have been brought down because of years-old unwise comments in their Twitter account!

If Joseph had risen to the heights he did in today's society, I wonder what would have been made of his boastful words, the words that displayed the mindset of a teenage boy. If he had thought that his words might come back to haunt him one day, I wonder if he might have been a little more humble?

The words we say matter – whether or not they might one day be used against us. Our words reflect what we believe and how we feel inside. Throughout the Bible, there are warnings about the importance of minding our words. Luke 6:45 reminds us: 'For the mouth speaks what the heart is full of.' Meanwhile Proverbs 6:2 talks about how you can be 'trapped by what you have said, ensnared by the words of your mouth'.

Joseph's careless words cause pain to his brothers, which turn into anger and bitterness towards him, leading to him being sold into slavery. We need to be careful about the words we speak. As Jesus followers, devoted to the *logos* – the Word, Jesus – we must be those whose lives reflect his love and that includes the words that come out of our mouths. Today, my prayer is that you would speak love and life and hope into the lives of those around you – your colleagues, your community, your family.

May the words of our mouths be pleasing to you, Lord God.

CHINE MCDONALD

The pit of despair

So when Joseph came to his brothers, they stripped him of his robe – the ornate robe he was wearing – and they took him and threw him into the cistern. The cistern was empty; there was no water in it. (NIV)

Life is full of ups and downs. One moment, Joseph was basking in the glory of his father's favouritism, complete with an ornate coat, and the next he had been thrown into a cistern in the wilderness – betrayed by his brothers. This must have been one of the darkest moments of his life. As we have seen, the early passages in the story of Joseph show he lacked a certain sense of self-awareness and was not sensitive to just how his brothers were feeling about him. It would have come as even more of a shock, therefore, for him to find himself in the bleak position he was in. Lost, alone, afraid, betrayed.

At times like this, it's so easy to lose all hope, to be so engulfed by despair that you cannot see a way through the fog of melancholy. And yet, in the depths of the pit, God can turn situations around. God can rescue us, just as he did with Joseph by sending the Ishmaelites his brothers decided to sell him to. But the thing about an incarnate God is that he is just that – God is right there with us in the pit, whether we are rescued or not. He does not allow us to suffer alone. He is not a God that is distant from our pain. He doesn't just hear our cries from afar, but he cries with us, holding our hands through our lowest moments. Our God is a God who never leaves us or forsakes us. He is our Immanuel. God with us on the rollercoaster of life – rejoicing in our joy and feeling our pain. May we be people who walk in the light of the amazing knowledge of God's incarnation.

When are the times in your life that you have felt God's presence with you the most? Thank God for his closeness to us through all things.

CHINE MCDONALD

True prosperity

And the Lord was with Joseph, and he was a prosperous man; and he was in the house of his master the Egyptian. And his master saw that the Lord was with him, and that the Lord made all that he did to prosper in his hand. (KJV)

In the King James Version of today's passage, Joseph is described as a prosperous man. The word 'prosperity', when used in the context of Christian teaching, is controversial. 'Prosperity gospel' is a pejorative phrase attached to some, especially TV evangelists, who profess faith in God but yet amass obscene amounts of material wealth. For these wealthy Christians, the money they have gained is a sign of God's favour upon them. God is, of course, the God of the rich as well as the poor. He is also able to do all things, including bless people financially. But there is a problem when prosperity is only linked to material wealth rather than spiritual. If prosperity meant nothing other than material wealth, then Joseph would not be described in today's passage as a prosperous man. From the outside world, he might not look prosperous. He is sold like cattle by his brothers to the Ishmaelites and is now a slave to Potiphar with no possessions of his own. It is Potiphar who might be the one described as prosperous: he is wealthy and influential, with the ability to purchase material possessions. But it is Joseph whom the Bible says is 'prosperous'.

Prosperity is about blessing and about flourishing. These are things that can only be truly found in and through God. St Augustine prayed: 'Lord… you have made us for yourself and our hearts are restless until they find their rest in you.' It is only in God that we find prosperity and an end to our searching. All good things come from him.

When you look at your own life, could you be described as a prosperous woman? Where are the areas of your life in which you see God's favour?

May you be reminded of your own prosperity today.

CHINE MCDONALD

Salt and light

The Lord was with Joseph so that he prospered, and he lived in the house of his Egyptian master. When his master saw that the Lord was with him and that the Lord gave him success in everything he did, Joseph found favour in his eyes and became his attendant. (NIV)

Have you ever been asked what it is that makes you different? Time and again, I have heard of Christians being asked at work or in other situations what it is they have that others haven't. It seems that non-believers often sense in the people of God some sort of inner peace or purpose; something they can't quite put their finger on. And they are often intrigued by it. What is it that makes these Christians different? It's not necessarily that we are nicer or kinder or more generous or loving – though we may strive to be all of these things. It seems that, when we are indwelt by the Holy Spirit, there is a certain mystery that surrounds us that causes people to ask questions.

And so it may have been for Joseph. Today's passage describes how God was with him so that he prospered in the house of Potiphar. Potiphar saw something special about him and the success that he had because of his unique relationship with God. Elevating Joseph to be in charge of his whole household meant that Potiphar's house also prospered.

Where the people of God are, there should be flourishing. It should make a difference that we are in the workplaces, communities and families in which God has placed us. We should pray that God would be with us, but also that he would be in those places. Wouldn't it be amazing if people saw every single Christian they work with in the way that Potiphar saw Joseph? He saw something special in him – not because of his own skills but because God was with him. Let us pray that we too are seen as salt and light that really makes a difference wherever we are.

How are you making a difference in the workplaces, communities and families in which God has placed you? Pray that God might continue to shine his face upon you, and that others will notice and be drawn to him.

CHINE MCDONALD

Immanuel: God with us

Joseph's master took him and put him in prison, the place where the king's prisoners were confined. But while Joseph was there in the prison, the Lord was with him; he showed him kindness and granted him favour in the eyes of the prison warden.' (NIV)

The number of Christians being persecuted around the globe for their faith is growing every year. All over the world, there are harrowing stories of Jesus' followers who refuse to renounce their faith and therefore face great horrors: execution, displacement, violence and hatred. Those of us in the west who profess a faith in God are likely not to experience our faith tested in such a way.

I have often wondered how unspeakably difficult it must be to have to choose between your faith and your life. But I have always been astounded by hearing stories of persecuted Christians in countries such as North Korea and Iran. Despite the persecution, the church around the world is growing, a church filled with people of immense faith. God is with them, just as he was with Joseph in prison. Today's passage describes how God is with him despite the circumstance in which he finds himself. In prison, God shows him kindness and grants him favour in the eyes of the prison warden guarding him.

Isn't it amazing the way God comes alongside those who are suffering? Whether it is those facing persecution because of their faith, or the many people I have known who have faced illness or tragedy, it never fails to astound me that time and time again these people talk about the way in which they have experienced God with them through it all.

What situation do you find yourself in today? Are you full of joy or are you facing turbulent times? Whatever you are facing this day, may God wrap his arms around you and may you feel his presence with you.

Hold me tight today, dear Lord.

CHINE MCDONALD

It's all in the timing

When Joseph came to them the next morning, he saw that they were dejected. So he asked Pharaoh's officials who were in custody with him in his master's house, 'Why do you look so sad today?' (NIV)

Joseph's encounter with Pharaoh's chief baker and cupbearer in prison and his subsequent interpretation of their dreams is key within this famous story. It shows the way in which so many strands to a story can come together at just the right time in just the right place. On the surface of it, Joseph has been imprisoned wrongfully, but it is in this place – in the midst of a perceived injustice – that God brings two characters into his life; and these characters will change the course of his life and set in motion significant changes to Israel's history.

But this isn't immediately apparent. There is a period of waiting. Pharaoh's cupbearer forgets all about Joseph once he is released – until Pharaoh's restless night's sleep jogs his memory about the dream interpreter he had once met. In those two full years in between, the thoughts that must have been running through Joseph's mind would be familiar to many of us who have experienced this waiting for a promise of God to come to pass. 'Will my situation ever change?' 'Did God really promise me that?' 'Why is it taking so long?'

In these situations, it's easy for doubt to replace faith. But God asks us to trust in him despite our lack of faith, despite not knowing the end of the story. For many years, God's promise to me that I would be married and have children felt like a joke as I saw my single years stretching out before me. But as I sit here writing with my newborn baby at my breast, I realise that God keeps his promises, just as he did for Joseph. It's just all in the timing.

What promises of God have you held on to, but have not yet come to pass? Make a list of them and ask God to fill you afresh with an unshakeable faith.

CHINE MCDONALD

Spirit-filled leadership

So Pharaoh asked them, 'Can we find anyone like this man, one in whom is the spirit of God?' (NIV)

Walk into any bookshop and you will notice that thousands of books have been written about leadership. These books line the shelves and promise organisations, businesses and nations the magic keys to being a great leader that will in turn bring about the profit, growth and flourishing that they are looking for. Christian authors also search for the best theories and ways of leadership as applied to the church. They don't need to look much further than Joseph.

Joseph was an outstanding leader and one from whom those in leadership positions can learn a lot – about servant-hearted leadership, about humility in leadership, about compassion in leadership. The account of his life also tells us so much about the ups and downs of leadership. But the most valuable lesson we learn is that Joseph was a Spirit-filled leader. Pharaoh recognises him as someone 'in whom is the Spirit of God'. He knows that it is only such a man who will be able to lead Egypt through the trials that are to come.

But what does it mean for those in leadership positions to be Spirit-filled? In my experience, it takes devotion, trust in God and a commitment to dwelling in his presence and learning from the greatest of all servant-leaders, Jesus.

Leadership doesn't, however, just mean heading up a church, organisation, business or even a nation. God has placed people just like us in leadership positions in our homes, in our communities and in our churches. Yet some of us lack the confidence to recognise the leadership call that has been placed upon our lives, even though they might not be high profile or visible like Joseph's. What does it mean for you today to be a Spirit-filled leader?

Who are the leaders in your life, your home, your church, your community or your nation? Pray that they might be filled with the Spirit of God and demonstrate the servant-hearted leadership of Jesus.

CHINE MCDONALD

Seeing is believing

They told [Jacob], 'Joseph is still alive! In fact, he is ruler of all Egypt.' Jacob was stunned; he did not believe them. But when they told him everything Joseph had said to them, and when he saw the carts Joseph had sent to carry him back, the spirit of their father Jacob revived. (NIV)

I will never forget the moment my son was born. After a long and difficult labour, we finally heard the cries we had long been waiting for. My husband tells me that the first words I uttered through my tears were: 'Is he a boy?' Indeed he was. It was a fact we had been told many weeks before and we had been mentally preparing ourselves for having a son. But I didn't quite believe it until I saw it. This is despite going through the whole antenatal process with scans and doctors confirming that he would indeed be a boy. It was not until I could confirm it with my very own eyes once he had been born that I truly believed it.

The Bible is full of people who are asked to have faith in what they have not yet seen – sometimes impossible things. For example, bearing children in old age, seeing dry bones live, the blind being given their sight and the dead raised to life. Or believing that the son you thought was dead is now the ruler of all Egypt, just as we read in today's passage. It's no wonder Jacob at first does not believe. But he eventually goes to Egypt to see for himself. Sometimes we are asked to believe what we cannot see, to have faith in things not yet visible. But we must remember daily that our God is the God of the impossible. Because of his great might and power, as well as his love for us, he is able to do far more than we can ask or imagine.

What are you believing God for today that is not yet apparent?

CHINE MCDONALD

Time to forgive

When Joseph's brothers saw that their father was dead, they said, 'What if Joseph holds a grudge against us and pays us back for all the wrongs we did to him?' (NIV)

I'm always amazed by the courage and grace of relatives and loved ones of murder victims who are able to forgive the perpetrators. It is astounding to me that people in the midst of such heartbreak and tragedy can utter the words: 'I forgive you.' In human terms, it would be understandable for them to hold the deepest grudge, to desire revenge on those who have taken the lives of people they love.

Despite my amazement at such acts of forgiveness, it never ceases to remind me that this kind of forgiveness is possible with God, who is not restricted to humanity's way of doing things. Our God is a God of mercy and forgiveness – even in the face of those who turn their back on him or reject his Son. And this God-given forgiveness is found in today's passage. Joseph, by all accounts, could have given his brothers a dose of their own medicine in their time of need. It is, after all, what they were expecting. But instead, to their surprise, he shows them profound mercy and (after a time of testing) speaks kindly to them.

This is a lesson to us all: to forgive those who have done wrong to us; to show kindness to them, despite the unspeakable acts they might have committed against us. Throughout the New Testament, we are told that we must forgive and forgive and forgive; turn the other cheek, pray for those who persecute us. Above all, we must love. Because love is what God is.

Bring to mind those whom you have held a grudge against and consider whether you might be able to let go of what they have done, and to forgive them.

CHINE MCDONALD

God intended it for good

'You intended to harm me, but God intended it for good to accomplish what is now being done, the saving of many lives.' (NIV)

When you are going through some of the most painful and difficult trials of life, you will often find someone comes alongside you and attempts to encourage you by telling you that God will work the situation for good. At times, those words are a comfort to us as we face these daunting times. But at other times, the words provide little comfort. Why couldn't God accomplish his purposes without the suffering that you are having to go through, you might ask. What is the purpose of this pain and is there any way that it can be avoided, we wonder.

When I have gone through such trials, it is often a long time afterwards that I recognise and see God's hand throughout. Hindsight, then, is indeed a wonderful thing. And so it is for Joseph in today's passage. He has come a long way since boasting to his brothers about his dreams, through being sold into slavery, working for Potiphar, being imprisoned and rising to political heights. It is at this point that he can see that God intended all of it for good. This is his testimony to his brothers in that moment: that God's promises do come to pass. He sees that God has done it not just for his own sake but to accomplish the saving of many lives. At times, it is so difficult for us to see beyond our own situations and our own pain that it is impossible for us to see what God is doing beneath the surface. How amazing to think that God can bring about immense good from our personal trials and tribulations!

Are you going through a difficult time? Or do you have a friend or relative who is? Pray that God will bring comfort in the midst of pain, and that he will work things together for good.

CHINE MCDONALD

From generation to generation

Joseph stayed in Egypt, along with all his father's family. He lived a hundred and ten years and saw the third generation of Ephraim's children. Also the children of Makir son of Manasseh were placed at birth on Joseph's knees. (NIV)

A short while ago, we travelled from London to the north of England to introduce our newborn son to his great-grandfather, who was celebrating his 90th birthday. It was a special time for all of us and it was so lovely to watch as my husband's grandfather looked in wonder at this brand-new life, knowing that he himself was in the latter stages of his. My own grandparents live in Nigeria and were so excited about the birth of our son. In Nigeria, where life expectancy is much lower, it is truly a blessing to see the arrival of your great-grandchildren. There is a profound gratitude that comes from seeing this next generation of your family being born.

In today's passage, Joseph has come a long way from his boastful, teenage years. He has lived a life full of ups and downs and has risen to prominent heights. He has experienced violence and loss and betrayal and hope and success *and* God's favour upon him. Now at 110 years old, he is at the end of his life and is able to look back and see how blessed he has been by God.

What a wonder it must be to experience the next generation of your children's children. How amazing to hold a newborn life in your hands as yours draws to a close. Only some us will live long enough to see a third generation, but however many God-given days we have, we are to live each day worthy of the faith to which we have been called; to walk hand in hand with God through the adventures, the ups and downs and twists and turns of life.

Lord, whether we live long lives or short ones, may our days glorify you.
CHINE MCDONALD

Old Testament prayers

Amy Boucher Pye writes:

How's your prayer life? Do you often brim with excitement over the thought of communicating with God, or can it sometimes feel like drudgery? Or somewhere in between? I've gone through various seasons when it comes to prayer. In my 20s, my prayer life took off, for I started to sense the Lord speaking to me. I resonated with what Oswald Chambers said in *My Utmost for His Highest*, 'Get into the habit of saying, "Speak, Lord," and life will become a romance.'

But I had to learn how to discern what was God's voice, and what wasn't. I experienced some knocks and hard times when I got things wrong, but I never wanted to lose the communion I experienced with God through his Holy Spirit. I turned not only to the New Testament, but also to the Old. I loved reading Isaiah, for instance, as I would write out the beautiful promises that God made to his people and make them my own. Over the decades, I've continued to appreciate the people in the first part of the Bible.

And thus, for these notes, I have loved turning to some Old Testament characters to explore their adventure of prayer. I think Christians often skip over the Old Testament. Instead, when we think of prayer, we might look to Jesus teaching his disciples to pray; or to his prayers after their last supper together; or to Stephen, the first martyr, and his long prayer right before he was killed; or to many of Paul's prayers for the churches he addressed. But our faith is poorer with the exclusion of what's often known as the Hebrew Bible. It's a rich source to encourage us as we pray.

In our fortnight together, I've highlighted various different types of prayer, including when people hide from God, bargain with him, lament over painful situations, ask for success, praise him, learn to hear his voice and bring every emotion to him. I hope that these examples will confirm to us that there's really no wrong kind of prayer. After all, God made us to communicate with him. He wants to hear from us, whatever state our heart is in.

May you experience a deepening of your faith as you express your love for God through prayer – and as you discern his loving response to you.

A strained conversation

But the Lord God called to the man, 'Where are you?' He answered, 'I heard you in the garden, and I was afraid because I was naked; so I hid.' (NIV)

'Did you get into the biscuits?' I asked one of my young offspring when they had been hiding from me. 'No,' the child replied, even though I could see a few crumbs around the cute little mouth. 'Are you sure?' I asked. 'Because I'd be more upset about you not telling the truth than you eating something that is off limits.' Then the child admitted the transgression and I gave the offender a hug!

Hiding after we've done wrong is nothing new; it goes back to Eve and Adam disobeying God in the garden of Eden when they ate from the tree that God had told them not to touch. Thus the first instance in the Bible of a conversation between God and his people unfortunately records our first parents' shame, having been deceived by the serpent. What was to be a relationship of complete openness, love and communion was shattered by the rebellion of the created.

God responds with consequences for their sin – that Adam will toil painfully in his work and Eve will experience pain in childbirth and a desire for her husband, who will rule over her. We may have heard many sermons about their sin and these punishments, but what we might have overlooked in this story is that God doesn't banish his people forever. The conversation continues, although no longer can Adam and Eve live in the garden of Eden. They move out of paradise, but they wear the clothes God fashioned for them and continue to communicate with him, as we will see.

When you've done something wrong, do you feel able to return to God?

Father God, I've sinned against you, in my thoughts, words and deeds. I'm sorry. Please help me return to you, that I might hear your loving affirmation.

AMY BOUCHER PYE

The God who sees

She gave this name to the Lord who spoke to her: 'You are the God who sees me,' for she said, 'I have now seen the One who sees me.' (NIV)

Abraham and Sarah are rightfully heroes of the Bible, but they were not without faults and sin. How they treated Hagar, their servant, we may find appalling.

In the time of Abraham, people understood human reproduction to entail the woman as only a carrier for a baby, with the man's sperm being the vital component that brought new life. This may help to explain why Sarah and Abraham resort to trying for an heir with him sleeping with Hagar (v. 2). With the benefit of hindsight, we know that Sarah will feel jealous of Hagar when the servant becomes pregnant – the thing that Sarah has longed for.

Because Sarah is in a position of power, she abuses Hagar, and the servant flees to the desert. I wonder if Hagar thinks she will die there. She doesn't, for God intervenes, sending his angel to encourage her. He tells her to go back to Sarah and submit to her, and that he will increase her descendants (vv. 9–10). What a hard task for her to return, knowing that Sarah despises her, but she goes knowing that God has seen her. She who was invisible and without rights was made visible by the all-seeing God.

God can intervene in our lives when we feel unseen and alone. Note that *he* initiated the conversation with Hagar – he sought her out. She therefore felt seen and validated. I believe God similarly seeks us out. We might not experience a vision or visitation like Hagar did, but we could receive his love through other means: his still, small voice speaking in a note from a friend, or a seeming coincidence that affirms he is with us. I pray this is so for you today.

Father God, you see me in all my sinfulness – my anger, bitterness, pride and selfishness. But you transform me, changing me from the inside out. Please continue your work today.

AMY BOUCHER PYE

Loving laughter

Abraham fell face down; he laughed and said to himself, 'Will a son be born to a man a hundred years old? Will Sarah bear a child at the age of ninety?' And Abraham said to God, 'If only Ishmael might live under your blessing!' (NIV)

Have you ever come down with a fit of the giggles at a completely inappropriate moment? Or blurted out something, when later you wished you'd held back from saying something daft? I wonder if Abraham, after he fell face down in laughter at God's great promise of making him into the father of many nations, wished he could have taken back his guffawing response.

We might think that, when we pray to God, we should be formal and reverent. Certainly there is a place for bowing before the great and mighty God, worshipping him for his mercy and might, but we see in this delightful interchange that God doesn't seem to mind Abraham being totally honest with him. After all, he answers Abraham with a gracious response, affirming that he will bear a son through his barren wife, a son he'll name Isaac, which means laughter. The very laughter that erupted from Abraham now becomes his beloved heir's name. God also acknowledges that he'll care for Ishmael, saying that he has heard Abraham's plea.

If your relationship with God feels cold, like you're distant from each other, why not consider how you could have fun with him? Yes, *fun*. Depending on your personality, that might mean taking a long walk in the countryside, asking God to reveal himself to you as you surround yourself in beauty; it might entail taking up some musical instruments like King David; losing yourself in dancing and song (see 2 Samuel 6:12–15); writing a funny poem; throwing a party; or something completely different.

In whatever ways you express your love for God, know that he runs towards you with outstretched arms, wanting you to enjoy his joy, peace and rest. What are you waiting for?

Lord God, you made us to bring you glory, and we do so when we are honest with you. Thank you that we can pour out to you every thought, fear and joy that we experience.

AMY BOUCHER PYE

The unseen God

Then the man bowed down and worshipped the Lord, saying, 'Praise be to the Lord, the God of my master Abraham, who has not abandoned his kindness and faithfulness to my master. As for me, the Lord has led me on the journey to the house of my master's relatives.' (NIV)

Sometimes we might feel like we're praying into an empty void, for we don't sense God's presence or his response. Those seasons can feel excruciatingly hard; I've experienced them, but have found that they don't last forever. At other times, in contrast, God's answers come thick and fast, as we see in the story of Abraham's servant finding a wife for his beloved son.

Abraham places a heavy burden on his servant in entrusting him to find a wife for Isaac from his people. The servant feels the weight of this commission, querying his master about what happens if his efforts meet in failure. I love that we can see how much Abraham's faith has grown and flourished in the years since he received God's promise to be the father of many nations, for he answers with the complete conviction that God will find just the right woman for his son.

I don't think the servant shares Abraham's confidence, for when he reaches Nahor, the first thing he does is to pray earnestly that God would give him success. I can hear the servant saying, 'Hey, Lord! I'm here, fulfilling my part of the task, so I'm really hoping you'll show up. Give me a sign in the form of a woman offering me water!' And God does – note that even before the servant had finished praying, Rebekah comes bearing a jug for water. The servant didn't forget to give praise to God for answering his prayers. No doubt his faith was enlarged that day.

Might you have some deep desires you could similarly present to God?

Lord God, you are the provider. You went ahead of that servant, preparing the way. Help me to approach you in confidence, knowing that you are a good and loving Father.

AMY BOUCHER PYE

Our saving help

'Save me, I pray, from the hand of my brother Esau, for I am afraid he will come and attack me, and also the mothers with their children. But you have said, "I will surely make you prosper."' (NIV)

My husband and I were driving along the motorway towards home, our young son behind us asleep in his car seat. All of a sudden, a car clipped the front side of our vehicle, sending us spinning. Time seemed to slow down as I pressed back into my seat, watching the world circle around. My first reaction was to cry out to God for help: 'Lord, please save us!' Amazingly, after turning around completely, we ended up at the side of the road, out of harm's way. The only injury was my husband's whiplash.

Often, we cry out to God for help when we're faced with danger or distress. We see Jacob facing trouble as he plans to meet his estranged brother Esau, from whom he stole their father's blessing. He is right to fear the meeting, for he hears that Esau has 400 men with him. He makes some precautions to protect his people and then prays earnestly to God, reminding the creator of the promises God has made to him while also expressing his lack of worth for receiving these gifts of kindness and faithfulness. Then he asks God directly to save him.

I believe that if we train ourselves to pray to our loving God every day and in all situations, then when we find ourselves in situations of extreme pressure, we'll almost reflexively turn to prayer. The habit we've cultivated in the ordinary times will arise in those that are extraordinary. And God will hear and answer us, according to his plans and wisdom – which we often won't fully understand this side of heaven.

May you know God's saving hand in all the moments of your life.

Lord God, you helped Jacob and Esau to reconcile – that which seemed impossible. Help me in the seemingly impossible areas of my life.

AMY BOUCHER PYE

A song of Moses

'The Lord is my strength and my defence; he has become my salvation. He is my God, and I will praise him, my father's God, and I will exalt him.' (NIV)

Moses heartens me. Here's a leader who starts out as a stammering man, too scared to speak, who employs his brother to be God's mouthpiece to the Israelites. Then, over time, as Moses witnesses the way God leads his people, he grows in faith and confidence. And when the Lord delivers the Israelites from Pharaoh and his armies who are bearing down on them – by the amazing miracle of parting the Red Sea – he erupts into a song of praise.

He says that God is his song, his strength and salvation, a warrior whom he will praise and exalt. He recounts the actions of God in hurling the chariots and soldiers into the sea. Then he pauses to wonder at God, asking if any other god could rival him. Truly, he concludes, the Lord is unrivalled and he will reign forever more.

It's worth examining Moses' song of praise, for we can follow his format in voicing our thanks to God. The more we proclaim that God is the one who gives us strength, the more we will believe it not only in our heads but in our hearts. We too can list the ways God has saved us, and in specific actions as Moses does. This will help us to affirm with Moses that there is no other God who is as good, gracious and loving as he is.

As a way of pondering passages of scripture, I like to form them into a poem of my own words. I know we don't all like to write, so this exercise may not be your favourite, but give it a try if you think it might be helpful. If not, might there be another way of digesting songs of praise to God, that you too might overflow in wonder and thanks?

Heavenly Father, you can part the waters and save me; you are my shield and right hand. May I always turn to you for help, and may I give you thanks.
AMY BOUCHER PYE

Bitter weeping

In her deep anguish Hannah prayed to the Lord, weeping bitterly. And she made a vow. (NIV)

Women can be cruel to each other. Looking on their rivals with disdain, they dangle their triumphs over them and breed discontent. I can remember vividly the pain of betrayal by a friend I trusted, or the time I as the subject of gossip. I felt particularly saddened that I felt this hurt from those who were supposed to be my sisters in Christ.

Hannah felt the pain of being barren, and heaped on top of that particular sorrow was the anguish she felt at the hands of her husband's other wife, Peninnah. The latter had children, and seemed to lord this over Hannah, provoking her 'till she wept and would not eat' (v. 7). Here, we see Hannah not only pouring out her sorrow to God, but also making a vow to him. If God answered her cries for a son, she would dedicate him to God's service.

These deep prayers can take all of our emotion and appear odd to onlookers, as was the case with Eli. He, in fact, thought Hannah was drunk. When she corrected him, he prayed for God's blessings on her. And indeed, God answered both of these prayers with the gift of a son for Hannah and Elkanah, whom they named Samuel. Again, the name had meaning: 'Because I asked the Lord for him.'

How often do we think we ought not to pour out our souls in anguish before the Lord? That maybe we're being too needy and we should just get on with our lives? Sometimes we do have to relinquish a dream or a desire, but at all times, the Lord will hear us as we call out to him. We can approach him in confidence, as Hannah did.

Father, Son and Holy Spirit, you love it when we come to you with our requests and praises. Show me what is in my heart, that I might lift it before you.

AMY BOUCHER PYE

God's still, small voice

The Lord came and stood there, calling as at the other times, 'Samuel! Samuel!' Then Samuel said, 'Speak, for your servant is listening.' (NIV)

As I wrote in the introduction, learning to discern the still, small voice of the Lord took me years and more than a few heartaches. I was delighted when I first sensed God's gentle whisper, which echoed his promises in scripture. But in my enthusiasm, I ran ahead of him, believing I had heard his voice when in fact, I hadn't. I had to learn to slow down and weigh what I was hearing against the Bible and the wisdom of trusted Christian friends.

Young Samuel had to learn to hear God's voice, especially because God didn't speak often then (v. 1). Again and again, Samuel presented himself to Eli, his master, thinking that the call was from him, not realising it was God. Finally, Eli realised that God was calling Samuel, and so he told him what to do. I wonder if Eli had an inkling that the Lord would deliver some kind of judgement through the young prodigy. In the morning, he didn't shy away from finding out what Samuel had learned.

Samuel's story reminds us that we don't always hear God correctly, and that we can be helped by more mature Christians. But it also shows us that God *does* speak to us! So often we simply don't slow down enough to hear him, or perhaps we are afraid of what he will say. Yet if we see him as a loving Father who cares for us so much that he would send his Son to live as one of us, we can trust him fully, listening with expectation.

I hope you will continue to grow in confidence in hearing and discerning God's loving voice.

Lord Jesus Christ, you take us to the Father. Open our hearts, minds and ears, that we would hear you as you dwell within us.

AMY BOUCHER PYE

Glory to God

'Praise be to you, Lord, the God of our father Israel, from everlasting to everlasting.' (NIV)

King David loved to pray, as we see in the prayer book of the Bible, the Psalms. A man of poetry and song, he grew in faith through the years of his life, especially after he sinned by killing Uriah the soldier after sleeping with his wife, Bathsheba (see 2 Samuel 11). God forgave and restored him, and used him mightily.

One of the last projects David longed to undertake was to build a temple to honour God and to welcome his presence with his people. But the Lord decided to give that task to David's son, Solomon, for God didn't want a warrior building the temple.

David seems to have accepted the decision well, assembling all of the materials for Solomon to undertake the project. In front of those gathered, he gives thanks for their great generosity and for God's goodness and faithfulness. He gives back all of the honour and glory to God, in words that have been echoed by God's people for millennia: 'Yours, Lord, is the greatness and the power and the glory and the majesty and the splendour, for everything in heaven and earth is yours' (v. 11).

When I'm feeling grumpy and ungrateful, I try to lift my spiritual 'funk' by reading some of the great prayers, such as this, in the Bible. I remind myself that God is God and I am not; I start to reorient my emotions by acknowledging that everything I have has been given to me by God. Putting the prayers of the great heroes of the Bible into my own words also helps to personalise them and make them heartfelt.

How could you praise the almighty God today?

Praise the Lord, my soul; all my inmost being, praise his holy name. Praise the Lord, my soul, and forget not all his benefits – who forgives all your sins and heals all your diseases (Psalm 103:1–3).

AMY BOUCHER PYE

Uncontainable God

'But will God really dwell on earth? The heavens, even the highest heaven, cannot contain you. How much less this temple I have built!' (NIV)

In studying for my MA in Christian Spirituality, I enjoyed a module dedicated to exploring the *Spiritual Exercises of Ignatius of Loyola*. Ignatius was a Spanish nobleman who was injured in battle and, when he was recuperating, experienced God through imaginative prayer focused on Jesus. Over the following years, he developed a programme of spiritual exercises, based on finding God in all things.

Where does God dwell? Indeed, can we find him in all things, as Ignatius did? King Solomon acknowledged the Lord's presence when he dedicated the new temple that God had entrusted him to erect for God's glory. A cloud of God's presence fell, and the priests couldn't do their duties because of it. Solomon turned his wonder at this visitation into prayer. He noted that even the heavens couldn't contain the great and mighty God, but yet God delighted to be with his people.

Solomon's prayer can remind us that an unlimited God still limited himself in Jesus, all because of his love for us. And after Pentecost, God sent the Holy Spirit to dwell in his people, bringing them (us!) comfort, joy and peace. The uncontainable God lives within us.

Does this make a difference to our lives? Yes! When we ask Jesus to live with us, he does. He'll never leave us. We can practise his presence at any moment of the day, calling to mind the mystery of his life within us. We can find his strength when we are weak; his comfort when we are lonely; his joy when we are despondent.

I like to place my hand on my heart as a reminder of God's presence living in me. Might you give that a try?

Lord Jesus Christ, you promised your friends that you would send the Holy Spirit to live in them. May I know the peace and joy that this Comforter brings, that I may pass it on to others.

AMY BOUCHER PYE

Those with us

'Oh no, my lord! What shall we do?' the servant asked. 'Don't be afraid,' the prophet [Elisha] answered. 'Those who are with us are more than those who are with them.' And Elisha prayed, 'Open his eyes, Lord, so that he may see.' (NIV)

One of my friends exudes faith. She depends on God in all areas of her life – relationships, work, money – in such an all-out way that I haven't often witnessed (and wish I could emulate). Whenever I'm with her, I'm encouraged to trust God more. She reminds me of Elisha, who asked God to open the eyes of those who were with him so that they could see what God was doing in the unseen realm.

This may be a familiar story to you; if it is, ask God to reveal something fresh to you today as you reread it. When I read it this morning, I became a bit emotional at the thought of all that we cannot see unless we ask God to open our eyes and hearts. Do we have faith to see and believe? If not, can we ask God to enlarge our faith?

Elisha was a prophet who believed that God would answer his prayers. When he faced seemingly impossible situations, he somehow glimpsed the help that God had lined up for him. He wanted to share this spiritual way of seeing with others, such as his servant. He knew, however, that he couldn't open his servant's eyes, but that God would need to: 'Open his eyes, Lord, so that he may see' (v. 17).

Whether we have only a little faith or rather a great faith, we can ask God to increase it. One way of doing that is through sharing our confidence in God with others. Praying together over areas in our lives and communities, and recording the answers as a way of documenting God's faithfulness, will build our belief in God's goodness. May he open our eyes to see the unseen reality!

Lord, often I feel that those against me are great and mighty. Open my eyes that I might see your armies who are fighting for me. Help me to share my faith and confidence with others.

AMY BOUCHER PYE

Unclean, redeemed

'Woe to me!' I cried. 'I am ruined! For I am a man of unclean lips, and I live among a people of unclean lips, and my eyes have seen the King, the Lord Almighty.' (NIV)

When we experience God's holiness, we realise our own sinfulness. It's like a red-hot light shines into the darkness in our lives, revealing the places where we have rebelled against God. The experience can be a painful one, but it can lead to cleansing and redemption.

The prophet Isaiah had such an experience when he saw a vision of the Lord seated on a throne, with the angels above him singing, 'Holy, holy, holy is the Lord Almighty.' In Hebrew, a superlative was derived by saying the word twice, so to hear that God is three-times holy was the ultimate expression. God's holiness overawed Isaiah, and he realised that he was ruined, 'a man of unclean lips'. He confessed his unworthiness in seeing the most holy God. How did the holy Lord respond? By keeping his distance? No. The angels cleansed him, taking away his guilt, so that he could be God's messenger.

And this is the promise when we pray a prayer of confession to our forgiving God – he will cleanse us from all of our sin and set us free to love him and share his message of good news with others. We don't have to remain in a state of not being worthy, for God removes our shame and guilt through the death of his Son, Jesus. We stand on his promises, knowing that we are worthy because he has made us so.

If you feel you're not serving God to your full capacity because of some shame that shackles you, ask the Lord to free you from these chains. He's in the business of freedom and redemption. Amen?

Lord Jesus Christ, Son of the living God, have mercy on me, a sinner.

AMY BOUCHER PYE

Complaints presented

You deceived me, Lord, and I was deceived; you overpowered me and prevailed. I am ridiculed all day long; everyone mocks me. (NIV)

Sometimes I feel like echoing my kids when they are complaining: 'It's not fair!' I would like to join in, but I refrain for, after all, I'm the adult! We might also carry this 'Keep calm and carry on' attitude into our relationship with God, thinking that we shouldn't lay out our complaints before him. I believe strongly, however, that God hears us when we share our laments and discouragements with him. (But I want to highlight also that we shouldn't make complaint the *only* way we relate to God.)

Look at the prophet Jeremiah. He had been falsely imprisoned and humiliated, all for God, and when he was released, he was not pleased. He lets out his list of complaints to God, including that standing up for the Lord has brought him 'insult and reproach all day long' (v. 8) and that his friends are all waiting for him to slip (v. 10). He doesn't hold back from telling God how he feels.

And yet in the midst of the complaints, he affirms the goodness of God, that the Lord is with him 'like a mighty warrior' (v. 11). He affirms that God won't let him down – even though shortly later he curses the day he was born. His emotions are all over the place, but at least he lets them out before the Lord, who can give him some objectivity and peace.

If you revert into an inner monologue about how unfair life is, why not speak out your thoughts to God? You can ask him to show you where your thinking is amiss while you seek his guidance, help and love. I believe he will answer your prayer.

Holy Spirit, you are an advocate for the downtrodden. You fight my case for me, with an eloquence I'll never have. Help me to trust in you fully and completely.

AMY BOUCHER PYE

Redemption

'I said, "I have been banished from your sight; yet I will look again toward your holy temple."' (NIV)

In the Old Testament, as we've seen, people wrestle with God. Jacob did so one night with an angel, coming out alive but with a wonky hip (Genesis 32:22–32). Moses said he couldn't speak for God and had his brother stand in (Exodus 4:16) but later asked God to have mercy on the Israelites (Exodus 32:31–32). As we saw yesterday, Jeremiah complained to God about the unfair treatment he received. The list goes on, including the last Old Testament prayer we will explore, that of Jonah.

Jonah is often known as the reluctant prophet, for he ran from God's call to speak to the people of Nineveh. He ran so far that he ended up in the middle of the sea, trying to hide from the Lord. That didn't happen; as you probably know, he ended up being thrown overboard and swallowed by a giant fish.

If you have the time, read again slowly through Jonah's prayer from the fish's belly. It shows the movement of the soul from despair to salvation. Jonah was 'hurled into the depths' but acknowledges that God has brought his 'life up from the pit'. He won't waste away, but will shout in grateful praise.

As we draw our time together to a close, think back over the last fortnight. Which of the prayers spoke to you most powerfully, and why? Which will you continue praying? Which didn't resonate? Do drop us a line and let us know of your experiences and insights; we love hearing from our readers.

May you know a deep relationship with God, as you sense his loving affirmation and guidance. May you always hear his voice. And may the Lord continue to bless you richly and deeply, making his face to shine upon you.

'Surely your goodness and love will follow me all the days of my life, and I will dwell in the house of the Lord for ever' (Psalm 23:6).

AMY BOUCHER PYE

Holy Week

Sandra Wheatley writes:

Here we are, almost at that 'turn in the road' as Lent moves us towards the events of Holy Week, the last week of Jesus' life: a week about which arguably more has been written, more songs sung and poems penned than any other week in history.

A third of the gospel narrative is devoted to this one week: Matthew 21—28; Mark 11—16; Luke 19—24 and John 12—20. Of the 89 chapters in the gospels, 29 speak of events of Holy Week – it is that important.

But how are you feeling today? For those of you who have followed certain disciplines such as abstinence through Lent, has it been a delight, or a chore and challenge? For others of us, has it caught us a little by surprise that Easter is almost here and we've not really had time to prepare for it? Like Christmas, Easter can be a little fraught – with children at home on their break, relatives to visit, friends to cater for or church events to attend and participate in. It can be a bit of a blur, can't it? Perhaps we're so very familiar with the Easter story that the enormity and thrill of it has become a bit blunted for us.

But it is my prayer that, even though this road may well be familiar, our journey together will be unique.

Jesus has taken me down many familiar roads, but then I find he does something different. Has he ever done that with you, surprised or overwhelmed you with a new realisation of who he is or what he has done? Who knows what will happen this week as we once again look at these events. Familiar though they may seem, there is always, for the seeking heart, something new to discover.

At the heart of Holy Week is a path. It's a path that commenced on Palm Sunday when Jesus rode on a donkey in majesty and lowly pomp. He went on to suffer and die for our sins, and since he rose from the dead, it has become the path Jesus rides into our hearts, through his word and Spirit.

The first Palm Sunday

'Look, the Lamb of God, who takes away the sin of the world!' (NIV)

There is something breathtakingly wonderful about this Palm Sunday, even beyond its significance as the day Jesus rode into Jerusalem on a colt fulfilling the prophecy of the coming of the Messiah in Zechariah 9:9.

This very day in the Jewish Calendar, 10 Nisan, was Lamb Selection day. This day commemorates the very first Passover when Moses commanded that each family select a year-old lamb without blemish or defect to be their Passover lamb (Exodus 12:3). Once selected, it was to be kept until 14–15 Nisan and inspected every day to ensure no blemishes appeared, and only then could it be sacrificed as their Passover lamb. The tradition had arisen that it was the first-born lambs from the fields around Bethlehem that were selected for Passover offerings in Jerusalem. Yes, from Bethlehem to Jerusalem!

So, as Jesus rode into Jerusalem, knowing he was going there to be sacrificed, many lambs were being led from Bethlehem to Jerusalem for sacrifice.

Jesus' arrival in Jerusalem four days before Passover isn't a coincidence, nor is the fact that he entered the city at the same time as the lambs. It was not by chance that the perfect Lamb of God was born in Bethlehem. God, the divine author, is wonderfully bringing together the old and the new covenants in the story of salvation.

It makes the hairs on the back of my neck tingle as I understand more fully the significance of this day: Old Testament prophecies are fulfilled as Jesus *the Lamb of God* enters Jerusalem.

There are no coincidences in this life of faith we walk; there is no road we take because of chance. Every step, every encounter you have today, is already known by God and he will be with you every moment.

My heart cries 'Hosanna' once again as I welcome you into my life, Lord.

SANDRA WHEATLEY

Turning the tables

'My house will be called a house of prayer for all nations.' (NIV)

Today's reading might at first give the impression that Jesus wasn't in a very good mood on this Monday morning! (Perhaps you aren't feeling kindly disposed to those around you today! Monday mornings can so often have that effect, and woe betide anyone or anything that gets in our way.)

The contrast between the humble way in which Jesus entered Jerusalem the day before and his actions today can seem a little difficult to comprehend.

Have a look at Isaiah 56:3–8 for a clearer understanding of the temple and its worship because that casts light on what Jesus was doing – and why.

The area of the temple Jesus cleared was the Court of the Gentiles, designated as the place where literally anyone could enter and pray. Anyone. But it had become a marketplace. What had begun as a service to facilitate worship – in making animals available for the sin-offering and changing money so that pilgrims could pay the temple tax – became a booming business for unscrupulous merchants and moneychangers.

Isaiah 56:3–8 gives a picture of the radically inclusive temple worship Jesus had in mind. No wonder he was offended when he saw the promise to the Gentiles, the poor and marginalised being denied. His actions were disturbing, radical and just. It wasn't just a 'cleansing', it was a reopening of the Court of the Gentiles to the inclusive love of God.

What about us? Are there tables for us to overturn today in his name? When I read Isaiah 56, I recognise my responsibility to help 'right the wrongs', to redress the injustices I encounter. But what about 'radical inclusivity'? Are there ways in which the church today needs to be more radically inclusive?

Are we extending the inclusive grace of God to all?

Father God, help me to follow in Jesus' footsteps and, in his name, extend his grace to all, especially the marginalised.

SANDRA WHEATLEY

How we pray and how we live

'Have faith in God.' (NIV)

When Jesus returned to Jerusalem, he faced a barrage of challenges from the Pharisees, the Sadducees and the teachers of the law. His attitudes towards issues such as marriage in heaven, paying taxes to Caesar and the source of his authority were closely scrutinised. He passes these stern examinations with flying colours, once again mirroring the scrutiny the Passover lambs faced each day of this week to ensure they were without blemish or fault.

But in the midst of all the pressure and antagonism from those who oppose him, Jesus ensures there is an important lesson for his disciples to learn on how to pray and how to give.

Jesus' response to Peter's observation concerning the fig tree he cursed the previous day seems simple: 'Have faith in God.' If we have faith in God, we will even move mountains! But then comes the instruction of how we pray: not only with faith, but also with a forgiving heart! If, as we pray, we're reminded of the need to forgive and then don't act upon it, it can be a greater obstacle to prayer being answered than any proverbial mountain. Faith and forgiveness go hand in hand. For the disciples, this will be a lesson they'll need to learn by the end of the week.

As Jesus sits in the Court of the Women after his long day, he 'people-watches'. Many rich people put their offerings into the temple treasury, but one poor widow catches Jesus' eye. He calls his disciples for their second lesson of the day – how we live. And how we give.

Jesus commended the widow: 'She, out of her poverty, put in every-thing' (12:44). Jesus knew just how much she gave and all that it meant.

Lord Jesus, may we bring whatever offerings we have today to you with this widow's attitude. Please have all of me.

SANDRA WHEATLEY

Anointed, prepared

'She did what she could. She poured perfume on my body beforehand to prepare for my burial.' (NIV)

Wednesday of Holy Week was quiet. Very quiet. Following Sunday's triumphal entry, the temple cleansing on Monday and Tuesday's 'interrogation' by the religious leaders, Jesus stays in Bethany with his friends Mary, Martha and Lazarus.

I can't help wondering how Jesus was feeling, knowing that in such a short while he would face betrayal, denial and desertion – and die the most excruciating death. Jesus did what many of us do: he found strength and comfort in the company of friends and those he loved. This is Jesus, the Son of Man, in the company of his friends. No more debates or confrontations with religious leaders; that was finished.

There are two people who play a significant part in this quiet day. The contrast in their reactions to Jesus are stark.

As Jesus is reclining at the table of Simon the leper, a woman (John's gospel says it is Mary; see John 12:3) approaches with an alabaster jar of perfume and pours it over his head. Jesus knew the significance of this action. He knew it was to prepare him for his burial. It was an extravagant act of devotion, a 'beautiful thing', Jesus said (v. 6). He also claimed that 'wherever the gospel is preached… what she has done will be told, in memory of her' (v. 9).

Judas and the disciples thought otherwise. 'Why this waste?' they ask indignantly.

Soon afterwards, Judas headed to the chief priests and agreed to betray Jesus. It is striking that to Mary, Jesus was worth everything she possessed; to Judas, he was worth only 30 pieces of silver.

The scene was set and, at the close of this quiet day, Jesus' body was anointed for burial and the plot to kill him was in place.

As today draws to a close, my prayer is that I too will have done all that I could for Jesus, as Mary did.

SANDRA WHEATLEY

A vigil; my vigil

'Stay here and keep watch with me.' (NIV)

For many years, as evening ends on Maundy Thursday, I begin a simple vigil. Jesus' words, 'Stay here and keep watch with me', are a compelling invitation to withdraw to a quiet place and to keep watch.

I head to my bedroom, light some candles, read the scriptures of the last supper, the washing of feet, the questions, the betrayal… and then I do as Jesus asked – I keep watch… and pray… and remember him in breaking some bread and drinking some wine.

I try to picture Gethsemane, with the disciples unable to keep awake and Jesus unable to sleep. And then I wonder just what Jesus will have experienced and the agony he felt that caused his sweat to fall as drops of blood as he prayed (Luke 22:44). His anguished plea to God the Father repeated again and again – 'May this cup be taken from me. Yet not as I will, but as you will' (v. 39) – never fails to rip into my heart.

But Jesus did drink from the cup. He embraced the will of God, rose to his feet from his anguished prayer and walked towards the sleeping disciples and his impending betrayal and arrest.

During my evening vigil this Maundy Thursday, I promise I'll hold my copy of *Day by Day with God* and will pray for you, our precious readers and my fellow contributors. I have no way of knowing what you are facing or what challenges or battles you are having in embracing God's will. But I've learned that the will of God will never take me where the grace of God cannot keep me, where the arms of God cannot support me or where the comfort of God cannot dry my tears.

Help us to do your will.

SANDRA WHEATLEY

It is finished

Jesus called out with a loud voice, 'Father, into your hands I commit my spirit.' When he had said this, he breathed his last. (NIV)

The events of Good Friday move along at a breakneck speed. Jesus faced six trials, three before the Sanhedrin, two before Pilate and one with Herod. It was Pilate who proclaimed, 'I find no fault in him.' It was the Sanhedrin who declared him guilty.

As well as the trials, there were Peter's denial, Judas' suicide and the crowd baying for his crucifixion and pleading for the release of Barabbas. Even before the agony of the cross, there was the brutality of the flogging at the hands of the Roman soldiers who ripped into his body with such venom and force that he was rendered unrecognisable (Isaiah 52:14). Finally, he staggered to Golgotha and his death.

When we gaze at the cross, what do we see – death and life, hate and love, violence and peace, accusation and forgiveness, sin and purity, brokenness and wholeness, destruction and restoration, defeat and victory? All is lost; yet everything is gained. The cruellest form of execution is now a symbol of abundant life. But there's more, because for each of us, all of us, Jesus' death is personal. He did this for you, for me.

As the sun stopped shining at midday, I wonder if it was then that he took upon himself the sins of the world. His cry of 'My God, my God, why have you forsaken me' (Mark 15:34) was the first time Jesus hadn't addressed God as 'Abba' (Father). The sins Jesus bore separated him from God the Father for the first time ever. For three hours, Jesus' physical agony was compounded by being totally separated from God. He did this for us.

And then he died, committing his spirit into the hands of God his Father. His work was done. It was finished.

Whether or not this is the first time you have followed these events, pause and consider his love for you in doing all that he did – to make it possible for you to know forgiveness and the healing of that ache deep within. For you.

SANDRA WHEATLEY

The day after

But they rested on the Sabbath in obedience to the commandment.
(NIV)

This 'sandwich-Saturday' always has an odd feel to it. Between the horrors of Good Friday and the exuberance and rejoicing of Easter Day, we're faced with silence in scripture.

Jesus' body had been laid in the tomb in the garden. The women, Mary Magdalene, Mary the mother of James and Salome (Mark 16:1), had prepared spices and perfumes ready to return the following day. Now they rested. They needed to.

Many of us will recall how it feels those hours and that first day after a loved one has died. Our world will never be quite the same; there's an absence, a sense of loss that defies description. Even if expected, the death of a loved one stops us in our tracks. Our world stops. Often it needs to.

For the disciples and the women, their 'resting' may have only been externally. What would their thoughts have been? Everything they'd hoped for in Jesus lay lifeless in a garden tomb. Were any of them really able to remember or understand his words recorded in Matthew 17:23 that he would rise again? Perhaps not. Their grief was overwhelming, their loss too immense. So, on this sabbath, they rested.

You may not have the opportunity to have a sabbath-rest today but, if you can, try to steal some moments and gather the events of this past week around you once again. Perhaps you'll have time to see again that all Jesus said he would do, he did; all you have been and are because of your commitment to him are as new today as they ever were. You are his, redeemed and safe.

Sometimes our faith can seem a little jaded and ground down by events and circumstance, but we will always have the promise of tomorrow – Easter Day. Hallelujah!

Lord Jesus, thank you for the hope for tomorrow. A new day, a new beginning (Psalm 30:5).

SANDRA WHEATLEY

Resurrection life

Sheila Jacobs writes:

Welcome to the time period between Resurrection Sunday and the ascension. Jesus is alive! He is who he said he was and he has confirmed who he claimed to be. His work is done. He has bought our freedom. We can have eternal life, resurrection life.

But what *is* resurrection life? Is it about going around healing the sick, overcoming the forces of darkness and seeing Jesus at work, setting people free? Yes. Is it also about seeing the transformation in our lives and the lives of others? Yes. And is it about walking as Jesus walked, forgiving people, acting in love? Oh, yes. And that's what we're going to be thinking about here: how to be disciples. What does it actually mean to follow Jesus, as he told Peter in John 21:22? How can we live that new life of love, and help people to so see Christ living in us that they are attracted to him and his teaching?

Outside the kingdom of God, there is chaos. But there is a door in chaos, and that door is Jesus. Once we are in the kingdom, we begin to walk as Jesus walked. But we can't do it in our own power. We need that resurrection life inside us. We need the power of the Holy Spirit – not just when we are praying for the sick, or for a much-needed change in a lost person's life, but also when we are struggling to forgive the one who has hurt us or not to judge that person we don't actually like.

Sometimes it is about giving God space: trusting him to work in and through us – allowing Jesus to 'leak out of us' to the person in front of us. It's about listening to God, waiting on him, encouraging others to seek him and experience him for themselves. The ultimate transforming power is his alone. And yet, he uses us.

The apostle Paul said that if Christ was not raised from the dead, our faith is useless (1 Corinthians 15:14). But Jesus is alive, and invites us to follow him. And as we choose to journey with him, he says he is with us always (Matthew 28:20).

I pray that, as you read the following notes, you are challenged, inspired and encouraged. Be blessed and enjoy a fresh encounter with the Holy Spirit!

He's alive!

Finally the other disciple, who had reached the tomb first, also went inside. He saw and believed. (They still did not understand from Scripture that Jesus had to rise from the dead.) (NIV)

People may tell us all kinds of things about Jesus but, unless we encounter God for ourselves, it can all just seem like 'wordy words'. Before I had an experience of Jesus, when I was in my mid-20s, he seemed very far away – I suppose I had 'head knowledge'. But when I said, in crisis, 'If you're really there, will you handle my life, because I can't handle it any more,' I felt a peace and joy that was beyond understanding. I just *knew* Jesus was real.

Jesus is alive! Just as the disciples discovered on that very first Resurrection Sunday, the tomb is empty. Jesus had accomplished what he had come to earth to do. He had lived a perfect life and laid it down for you and me, so that we can be friends with God. Romans 3:23 tells us that we all come short of God's standard. By ourselves and our own efforts, we could never get right with God; none of our righteous acts would make us acceptable (Isaiah 64:6). It's by grace, God's free favour, that we are made right with him. We are all made in his image, but something went terribly wrong, as we read in the book of Genesis. But now, if we take that step of faith and receive Jesus, he gives us the right to become his children (John 1:12).

When the disciples peered into the empty tomb, they may not have understood how, or why, or what, or when. But we read that 'the other disciple' – probably the writer of the gospel – believed. That's all it takes. *All?* Is it easy, then? Maybe not. It's humbling to come to God and say: 'I've messed up. I want to know you. Please save me.'

If you have time, listen to Jesus Culture's 'Revelation Song' (or sing another song to him). Happy Resurrection Sunday!

SHEILA JACOBS

It's personal

'They have taken my Lord away,' [Mary] said, 'and I don't know where they have put him.' At this, she turned round and saw Jesus standing there, but she did not realise that it was Jesus. (NIV)

The others have gone home; Mary Magdalene is still at the empty tomb. It is she who has discovered that the Lord's body is missing, and we can only begin to imagine her grief; we know that Jesus has done much in her life to set her free (see Luke 8:2). This precious follower of Jesus is weeping, peering into the darkness – and then sees two angels. She talks with them, and turns. And then she notices a man.

Well, encountering angels is amazing to start with. To chat with them, even in these circumstances, would be mind-blowing. Perhaps that's why, when Mary turns round, she doesn't recognise Jesus. Or maybe his appearance is different. At any rate, she doesn't know immediately who he is – until he says her name. Then it's another story. Grief is turned to incredulity, and then, I expect, overpowering joy.

Grief, rejection, illness, life's events – all can hide the mystery of who Jesus is.

Mary's tears blinded her, and sometimes the events of life can blind us too to the one who stands in front of us and speaks our name. All too often, we as Christians can live a sort of Easter Saturday life, knowing Jesus died for us, but not fully living the kind of resurrection life that he died to bring us. The life Jesus promises us, a full life (John 10:10) is not always as we imagine it to be. It's not always about health and prosperity here and now. But it is about a quality of being that is different to anything we have known before. Today, let's remember that Jesus really is alive – not dead. We can have relationship with him; we can speak to him and hear him whisper our name. It's personal.

Imagine you are at the empty tomb with Mary. Jesus speaks your name. How will you respond?

SHEILA JACOBS

Disillusioned?

As they talked and discussed these things with each other, Jesus himself came up and walked along with them; but they were kept from recognising him. (NIV)

Here are two more disciples who don't recognise Jesus! Clearly, his resurrected body is very different; and yet, oddly, the same, for they *did* recognise him eventually – and he is still able to eat, as we see from Luke's account. Indeed, he seems keen to prove at that point that he isn't a 'ghost' (Luke 24:39–43). But just like Mary in yesterday's reading, the disciples 'see' but don't see.

If you are a Christian, have you ever been disillusioned with everything you thought you believed in? You can almost feel the tangible waves of disappointment from the two disciples on the Emmaus road. A 'stranger' begins to walk alongside them as they discuss what they have witnessed. They tell this stranger, who seems to know nothing of what has happened, about Jesus of Nazareth: that their hopes had been in this Jesus, whom they believed would 'redeem Israel'. (Actually, he did, but not as they expected.) He's dead. Yet some women have said they've seen a vision of angels who told them Jesus is alive. What confusion!

Jesus sometimes doesn't act as we expect him to. And that can leave us feeling disillusioned, doubting he is the one we thought him to be. We don't recognise him in the middle of our anguish and disappointment. But, maybe a lot later on, we understand that he was there all the time; we just didn't 'see' him.

That can be true too for those who don't yet know him. That grace-full presence may not be fully recognised for many years. Then, one day, we realise that the gentle knocking on our door is the sound of the very one who has been ardently pursuing us for a long, long time (Revelation 3:20).

Lord Jesus, help me to recognise you more in my daily life. Allow me to sense your gentle Spirit as you walk beside me, guiding and leading. Help me to recognise your voice and respond to you today.

SHEILA JACOBS

The real Jesus

And beginning with Moses and all the Prophets, he explained to them what was said in all the Scriptures concerning himself. (NIV)

Our version of Jesus doesn't always stack up with what is presented in the Bible. 'Oh, Jesus understands when I sin.' Hmm…!

On the road to Emmaus, the disciples are walking along with a man who doesn't seem to know anything of what has happened to the one they believed would redeem Israel, but he now begins to reveal who he is through the scriptures. Time spent with Jesus often results in us wanting more, and they ask him to stay with them. And then, of course, they at last see who he really is.

That he disappears is strange and awesome. But that he is alive is not in question. And how did he reveal himself? Through opening up the scriptures which pointed to him, before breaking the bread; his body, broken for them and for us.

It is so easy to stop reading the Bible, isn't it? When life gets busy, our Bible reading is one of the first things to be shelved if you're anything like me. And yet it is here that we get to know the real Jesus and see how he interacts with God and humanity. We might not like everything we read, but it will challenge as well as inform and encourage us.

Jesus comes alongside and shows himself to the two disciples; in a similar way, in John 4, we see him coming alongside the unnamed woman at the well, knowing all her 'issues', but not condemning – instead, he offers her something better. He offers her the living water of resurrection life. This is the all-powerful, real Jesus who calls us to follow him. What does that look like for you and me? God has good plans for us, but his ultimate plan is to make us like his Son!

Is your 'version' of Jesus the real one? Can you put some time aside today to read more from a gospel?

SHEILA JACOBS

129

Peace with God

Again Jesus said, 'Peace be with you! As the Father has sent me, I am sending you.' And with that he breathed on them and said, 'Receive the Holy Spirit.' (NIV)

In his first appearance to the disciples after his resurrection, Jesus says, 'Peace!' The disciples were obviously in great fear. But Jesus speaks loving, gracious words.

I was unwell recently, and unable to keep up my usual activities for a couple of weeks. While I didn't enjoy being poorly, I certainly benefited from the rest! I felt way more relaxed than I usually do. But real peace comes from the inside – peace with God. While I was resting, I spent some time just listening to the Lord, and was able to 'be still and know' (Psalm 46:10). Undistracted, I began to think about how Jesus was wounded for me. And I saw, perhaps with more reality than I had before, that when he died and rose again, he redeemed my whole life. My sins were forgiven. Not just yesterday's sins, but *all* of them. I myself was redeemed, from cradle to grave. When I didn't know him I was spiritually dead, but now I am spiritually alive. I have peace with God, life because of Jesus. The Spirit of God lives in me and is making me more like him.

The more we let go, the more we surrender, the more peace we feel. It isn't easy, because life, as we know, is stressful. But what I started to do when I was ill, I try to continue. Each evening, I find things to thank God for from the day and ask him what the day meant from *his* perspective. I've been surprised to find that he points out what I've done right – not the things I've got wrong (I repent of those later). God wants to put a tick in our box. Let's be keen to put a tick in each other's boxes too.

Lord, help me to find time to just be still and to know your peaceful presence today. Thank you, Jesus.

SHEILA JACOBS

Have faith

Thomas said to him, 'My Lord and my God!' Then Jesus told him, 'Because you have seen me, you have believed; blessed are those who have not seen and yet have believed.' (NIV)

It seems Thomas was not with the disciples a week earlier, when Jesus appeared to them for the first time. Famously, he doubted. But when presented with physical evidence, he utters the words of faith: 'My Lord and my God!'

A serious theological error is when people believe that Jesus is a great teacher, a great prophet or even a mighty angel, but not 'God in a body'. The revelation comes when we realise that Jesus is a man but more than a man; he is the exact representation of God's being (Hebrews 1:3): 'For in Christ all the fullness of the Deity lives in bodily form' (Colossians 2:9). Jesus, in John 8:58, equates himself with deity by referring to himself as 'I am', the name God revealed to Moses in Exodus 3:14. For that declaration, Jesus was nearly stoned for blasphemy.

Why does Jesus need to be fully God as well as fully man? Because only a perfect man could fulfil God's law and lay down that sinless life on behalf of others. And only God is perfect.

Jesus came to show us what God is like – to make him known (John 1:18). We can't explain the mystery of the Trinity. But there are three that are one.

As the result of his encounter with Jesus, Thomas believed. But Jesus said that those who didn't see with their natural eyes would be blessed because they believed by faith. Sometimes, when life seems difficult, we may not feel as if we are experiencing resurrection life. It's at times like this that we need to spend time thanking God and praising him *despite* our feelings. Feelings can lie to us; Jesus is the truth.

Father, at times my faith feels weak. Let me remember then to look to your Son, remember who he is and what he has done, and praise you!

SHEILA JACOBS

No condemnation

When they had finished eating, Jesus said to Simon Peter, 'Simon son of John, do you love me more than these?' 'Yes, Lord,' he said, 'you know that I love you.' Jesus said, 'Feed my lambs.' (NIV)

What do you do when someone lets you down? Do you seethe with anger? 'You wait! I'll get my own back!' I guess that's natural – but it isn't living the resurrection life.

Peter had denied Jesus, letting his friend down badly. What kind of reaction might he have expected from the resurrected Christ? Rejection? 'Call yourself a disciple? You disgust me!' No. This third time Jesus meets with the disciples after his resurrection, he cooks breakfast and asks Peter if he loves him. The reinstated Peter will be taking care of the church. This is true forgiveness – real love.

When we claim to walk as Jesus did, we must live in love (1 John 2:5). How hard it is, sometimes, to let go of the past and of real or imagined hurts. But I'm sure you have heard the saying – unforgiveness is like drinking poison and expecting our enemy to die. Harbouring resentment only damages *us*. We ask, 'Why should I let that person off the hook?' but forgiving lets *us* off the hook so that we can walk forward into the new life that God is bringing us.

If we are followers of Jesus, we must do as he did: forgive and, where possible, restore (although that might not always be safe or wise). Our pain may be valid, but we need to trust God with it.

When we are the ones who mess up and come to him, God gently restores us. No condemnation. We may expect criticism or blame, especially if this is how significant figures in our lives have treated us in the past. But remember the story of the prodigal son in Luke 15 – and the Father's love? The prodigal may have been covered in pig poo, but he was still a son!

Do you want to walk forward with Jesus? Is there anyone you need to forgive – or restore? Maybe it is you who needs forgiveness. Come to Jesus now. He loves you.

SHEILA JACOBS

It's in the mind

When Peter saw him, he asked, 'Lord, what about him?' Jesus answered, 'If I want him to remain alive until I return, what is that to you? You must follow me.' (NIV)

Have you ever been around Christians who have 'pointed the finger'? Easy to do, isn't it? 'Oh, she doesn't go to *any* of the prayer meetings.' (She's at home looking after two kids, exhausted, with her husband working long hours.) 'Oh, he *never* does outreach with us.' (No, he suffers from chronic shyness but spends two hours each night on his knees praying – a thing he'll never tell you.) How very easy it is to judge – when we don't know all the facts!

A part of resurrection life is learning not to point the finger or to fix our eyes on what other people might be doing (or not doing). Here, Peter, as he walks with Jesus, looks at another disciple and asks, 'What about him?' Jesus answers, in effect, 'You follow me! Concentrate on your own walk!'

Recently, I found myself 'judging' others in my heart. I felt a rebuke from the Lord: 'When did you stop loving?' But it isn't always easy to love. Sometimes, we can wonder how it is possible at all – depending on the person and the state of our own heart. If we equate love with 'doing', we might find it hard to show our love if we are restricted through illness or other life circumstances – or if the person we want to show love to simply won't or can't receive it. So how can we love, when we cannot always 'do'? Well, we can love others *in our mind*, praying for and blessing them, not allowing negative thoughts to fester – which often leads to an overflow of the mouth, when we just can't resist criticising.

It all happens in the mind first. We need to decide to follow Jesus in our thought-life.

Loving heavenly Father, help me to take all my thoughts captive and to live a life of love, just as your Son did. Help me to pray and to think kindly.

SHEILA JACOBS

Letting go

'Go and make disciples of all nations, baptising them in the name of the Father and of the Son and of the Holy Spirit, and teaching them to obey everything I have commanded you.' (NIV)

Here we read the 'great commission'. Jesus tells his followers that they must go and teach others to obey all that he has commanded them.

If we love Jesus, we will obey him. So, what *are* his commands? In John 15:17, we read that his command is that we love each other.

Love each other! And teach others to love! If we read the gospels and see how Jesus interacted with people, and understand that he says 'go and do likewise', we may throw our hands up in despair. How can we act in love towards people – yes, even other Christians! – who may have hurt us?

If we think we can make ourselves like Jesus by our own power, we are mistaken. If we believe we can transform others, we are also in error. It is the Spirit who transforms lives.

In Luke 24:46–49, Jesus speaks of his followers being 'clothed with power from on high'. We may think that supernatural power is all about healing the sick, delivering people from all manner of darkness and doing miracles – and yes, that is a part of living the Christ-life (see Mark 16:9–19). But there is a quieter aspect to the supernatural resurrection life, as we trust the Holy Spirit day by day to empower us to react as Jesus did to life's events and crises, and to treat people as he would treat them.

When I was incapacitated with Ménière's disease and agoraphobia, more than 20 years ago, I said to God: 'All I wanted to do was work for you.' He replied, 'I don't want you to work for me. I want to do my work in and through you.' That's when I began to see that following Jesus is all about letting go.

Lord Jesus, help me to 'let go' so you can do your work in and through me. I want to love others and teach them, too, to love.

SHEILA JACOBS

Run to him

'Wait for the gift my Father promised, which you have heard me speak about. For John baptised with water, but in a few days you will be baptised with the Holy Spirit.' (NIV)

Yesterday we thought about the great commission. Where Jesus commands, he equips. About to ascend to heaven, he told his disciples to wait for 'the gift' his Father promised. What gift? The gift of the Spirit… the gift that would enable them to live the Christ-life and to disciple others. What makes somebody a Christian with resurrection life within? The Holy Spirit, that life-giving water Jesus spoke about in John 4. And the call is to 'follow me' – to walk as he walked and to share what we have experienced of him. Evangelism is all about introductions – encouraging people to encounter God for themselves. As they do, we are invited to journey together.

The ascension itself is shrouded in mystery, but we know that Jesus will one day return 'in the same way'. In the meantime, he is interceding for us at the right hand of God (Romans 8:34). He has walked the earth as a man, 'been tempted in every way' (Hebrews 4:15) and so, wonderfully, can sympathise with us. He understands when we are disappointed, have messed up or are simply longing for 'something more'. We can have full assurance that he will not reject us when we come to him with our hopes, our requests and our failures. So often, when we're in need, we run *from* God, rather than running *to* him!

Let's turn to Jesus in our frailty, trusting him to equip us with resurrection life, so we can live in his presence, radiating who he is to a world that, largely, doesn't recognise him. We have a message of life – his message, his life, lived out in his power.

One day, Jesus will return. But until that time, as God gives us grace. We need to be about our Father's business!

Father, thank you for sending your Son so I may have resurrection life. Thank you for the gift of the Holy Spirit, who empowers me to live it. I love you, Lord!

SHEILA JACOBS

Recommended reading

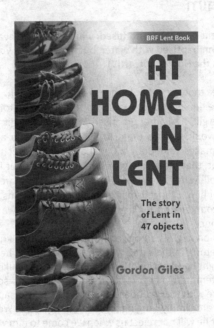

Here is an original way of approaching Lent, one that will encourage you to consider your own faith journey in the light of the Easter story. Gordon Giles spends each week in a different room gleaning spiritual lessons from everyday household objects. As a result, you might discover that finding God in the normal pattern of life – even in the mundane – transforms how you approach each day.

At Home in Lent
The story of Lent in 47 objects
Gordon Giles
978 0 85746 589 4 £8.99
brfonline.org.uk

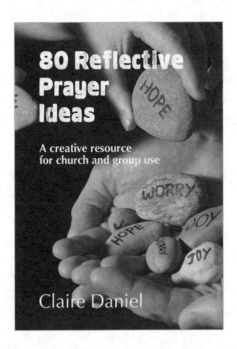

Prayer remains a vital part of Christian discipleship. Following the success of the author's *80 Creative Prayer Ideas*, this ready-to-use resource book contains 80 further ideas on setting up reflective and creative prayer stations or responses. Claire Daniel shows us how to pray with our whole being – our senses as well as our voice, our hearts as much as our minds. Tried and tested, these ideas will enhance the praying of small groups, churches and individuals.

80 Reflective Prayer Ideas
A creative resource for church and group use
Claire Daniel

978 0 85746 673 0   £12.99
brfonline.org.uk

Collecting all the wisdom of titles previously published as *Parenting Children for a Life of Faith*, *Parenting Children for a Life of Purpose* and *Parenting Children for a Life of Confidence*, this book provides inspiration and wisdom for nurturing children into the reality of God's presence and love. It equips parents to help their children to access God themselves and encourage them to grow in a two-way relationship with him that will last a lifetime.

Parenting Children for a Life of Faith (Omnibus Edition)
Helping children meet and know God
Rachel Turner
978 0 85746 694 5 £12.99
brfonline.org.uk

This inspirational book takes the reader through the 40 days of Lent to the celebration of Easter through the eyes and beliefs of Celtic Christianity. Drawing on primary sources of pastoral letters, monastic rules and the theological teaching of the Celtic church, the author presents a different perspective on the cross of Christ and draws us to see our own life journeys with a new and transforming vision.

Celtic Lent
40 days of devotions to Easter
David Cole
978 0 85746 637 2 £8.99
brfonline.org.uk

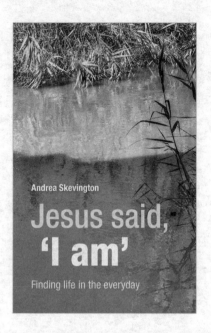

Drawing on the imagery of the Hebrew scriptures, Jesus identifies himself as the 'I am' of Israel's narrative. Through sensitive retelling, thoughtful discussion and creative exercises, Andrea Skevington shows the transforming power of Jesus' words. *Jesus said, 'I am'* integrates faith and imagination, story and study, helping readers towards a well-grounded and more profound faith.

Jesus said, 'I am'
Finding life in the everyday
Andrea Skevington
978 0 85746 562 7   £8.99
brfonline.org.uk

To order

Online: **brfonline.org.uk**
Tel.: +44 (0)1865 319700
Mon–Fri 9.15–17.30

Delivery times within the UK are normally
15 working days. Prices are correct at the time of
going to press but may change without prior notice.

Title	Price	Qty	Total
At Home in Lent	£8.99		
80 Reflective Prayer Ideas	£12.99		
Parenting Children for a Life of Faith (Omnibus Edition)	£12.99		
Celtic Lent	£8.99		
Jesus said, 'I am'	£8.99		

POSTAGE AND PACKING CHARGES			
Order value	UK	Europe	Rest of world
Under £7.00	£2.00	£5.00	£7.00
£7.00–£29.99	£3.00	£9.00	£15.00
£30.00 and over	FREE	£9.00 + 15% of order value	£15.00 + 20% of order value

Total value of books	
Postage and packing	
Total for this order	

Please complete in BLOCK CAPITALS

Title _____ First name/initials _____ Surname _____

Address _____

_____ Postcode _____

Acc. No. _____ Telephone _____

Email _____

Method of payment

☐ Cheque (made payable to BRF) ☐ MasterCard / Visa

Card no. ☐☐☐☐ ☐☐☐☐ ☐☐☐☐ ☐☐☐☐ ☐☐☐☐ ☐☐☐☐

Valid from ☐☐ ☐☐ Expires ☐☐ ☐☐ Security code* ☐☐☐

Last 3 digits on the reverse of the card

Signature* _____ Date _____ /_____ /_____

*ESSENTIAL IN ORDER TO PROCESS YOUR ORDER

Please return this form with the appropriate payment to:
BRF, 15 The Chambers, Vineyard, Abingdon OX14 3FE | enquiries@brf.org.uk

To read our terms and find out about cancelling your order, please visit **brfonline.org.uk/terms**.

The Bible Reading Fellowship is a Registered Charity (233280)

SUBSCRIPTION INFORMATION

Each issue of *Day by Day with God* is available from Christian bookshops everywhere. Copies may also be available through your church book agent or from the person who distributes Bible reading notes in your church.

Alternatively you may obtain *Day by Day with God* on subscription direct from the publishers. There are two kinds of subscription:

Individual subscriptions
covering 3 issues for 4 copies or less, payable in advance (including postage & packing).

To order, please complete the details on page 144 and return with the appropriate payment to: BRF, 15 The Chambers, Vineyard, Abingdon OX14 3FE

You can also use the form on page 144 to order a gift subscription for a friend.

Group subscriptions
covering 3 issues for 5 copies or more, sent to **one** UK address (post free).

Please note that the annual billing period for group subscriptions runs from 1 May to 30 April.

To order, please complete the details on page 143 and return with the appropriate payment to: BRF, 15 The Chambers, Vineyard, Abingdon OX14 3FE

You will receive an invoice with the first issue of notes.

All our Bible reading notes can be ordered online by visiting
biblereadingnotes.org.uk/subscriptions
For information about our other Bible reading notes,
and apps for iPhone and iPod touch, visit
biblereadingnotes.org.uk

All subscription enquiries should be directed to:
BRF, 15 The Chambers, Vineyard, Abingdon OX14 3FE
+44 (0)1865 319700 | enquiries@brf.org.uk

DAY BY DAY WITH GOD GROUP SUBSCRIPTION FORM

All our Bible reading notes can be ordered online by visiting
biblereadingnotes.org.uk/subscriptions

The group subscription rate for *Day by Day with God* will be £13.80 per person until April 2020.

☐ I would like to take out a group subscription for .... (quantity) copies.

☐ Please start my order with the May 2019 / September 2019 / January 2020* issue.
I would like to pay annually/receive an invoice* with each edition of the notes.
(*delete as appropriate)

Please do not send any money with your order. Send your order to BRF and we will send you an invoice. The group subscription year is from 1 May to 30 April. If you start subscribing in the middle of a subscription year we will invoice you for the remaining number of issues left in that year.

Name and address of the person organising the group subscription:

Title .... First name/initials .... Surname ....

Address ....

.... Postcode ....

Telephone .... Email ....

Church ....

Name of Minister ....

Name and address of the person paying the invoice if the invoice needs to be sent directly to them:

Title .... First name/initials .... Surname ....

Address ....

.... Postcode ....

Telephone .... Email ....

Please return this form with the appropriate payment to:
BRF, 15 The Chambers, Vineyard, Abingdon OX14 3FE

To read our terms and find out about cancelling your order, please visit **brfonline.org.uk/terms**.

The Bible Reading Fellowship is a Registered Charity (233280)

DAY BY DAY WITH GOD INDIVIDUAL/GIFT SUBSCRIPTION FORM

To order online, please visit **biblereadingnotes.org.uk/subscriptions**

☐ I would like to give a gift subscription (please provide both names and addresses)
☐ I would like to take out a subscription myself (complete your name and address details only once)

Title _____ First name/initials _____ Surname _____

Address _____

_____ Postcode _____

Telephone _____ Email _____

Gift subscription name _____

Gift subscription address _____

_____ Postcode _____

Gift message (20 words max. or include your own gift card):

_____

_____

Please send *Day by Day with God* beginning with the May 2019 / September 2019 / January 2020 issue (*delete as appropriate*):

(please tick box)	UK	Europe	Rest of world
1-year subscription	☐ £17.40	☐ £25.50	☐ £29.40
2-year subscription	☐ £33.00	N/A	N/A

Total enclosed £ _____ (cheques should be made payable to 'BRF')

Please charge my MasterCard / Visa ☐ Debit card ☐ with £ _____

Card no. ☐☐☐☐ ☐☐☐☐ ☐☐☐☐ ☐☐☐☐

Valid from ☐☐ ☐☐ Expires ☐☐ ☐☐ Security code* ☐☐☐

Last 3 digits on the reverse of the card

Signature* _____ Date _____/_____/_____
*ESSENTIAL IN ORDER TO PROCESS YOUR ORDER

Please return this form with the appropriate payment to:
BRF, 15 The Chambers, Vineyard, Abingdon OX14 3FE

To read our terms and find out about cancelling your order, please visit **brfonline.org.uk/terms**.

The Bible Reading Fellowship is a Registered Charity (233280)

DBDWG0119